W9-BAG-526

KEYS TO INVESTING IN YOUR 401(K)

Second Edition

Warren Boroson
Instructor,
The New School;
Financial Columnist,
Morristown (N.J.) *Daily Record*

BARRON'S

© Copyright 2000 by Barron's Educational Series, Inc.
Prior edition © Copyright 1994 by Barron's Educational Series, Inc.

All rights reserved.
No part of this book may be reproduced in any form, by photostat,
microfilm, xerography, or any other means, or incorporated into any
information retrieval system, electronic or mechanical, without the written
permission of the copyright owner.

All inquiries should be addressed to:
Barron's Educational Series, Inc.
250 Wireless Boulevard
Hauppauge, New York 11788
http://www.barronseduc.com

Library of Congress Catalog Card No. 00-31245

International Standard Book No. 0-7641-1298-8

Library of Congress Cataloging-in-Publication Data

Boroson, Warren.
     Keys to investing in your 401(k) / Warren Boroson.—2nd ed.
        p.   cm. — (Barron's business keys)
     Includes index.
     ISBN 0-7641-1298-8
     1. 401(k) plans. I. Title. II. Series.

HF5549.5.C67 B67 2000
332.024'01—dc21   00-31245
                                                                      CIP

PRINTED IN THE UNITED STATES OF AMERICA

9 8 7 6 5 4 3 2 1

TABLE OF CONTENTS

1

MISTAKES WITH 401(K) PLANS

A 401(k) plan is so vital to your being able to retire comfortably, so essential to your financial health in general, that the most important thing for people who can invest in such plans to know, first off, is what mistakes they should avoid making.

First and worst mistake: to invest in volatile securities (like stocks), then to sell in a panic if their prices decline.

To put it another way, the worst mistake is for a novice to make an investment suitable for sophisticated investors. Stocks may be wonderful investments—for sophisticated people. Guaranteed investment contracts (Key 33) may be inappropriate investments for sophisticated people—but not for novices.

No other mistake can prove so costly as buying volatile securities if you aren't prepared to cope with volatility—whether the other mistake is investing too conservatively, not investing enough, whatever.

Second common and expensive mistake: not taking advantage of a 401(k) plan when people have one available. Right now, only 78 percent of those Americans eligible for 401(k)s have chosen to participate. Twenty-two percent of the people eligible are missing out on one of the truly golden opportunities of their lives.

Unfortunately, the well-to-do are more likely to participate than the less well-to-do, who would probably benefit more. By and large, the higher-paid an employee covered by a 401(k) plan is, the more likely that person is to salt money away into a plan. Someone earning over

$50,000 a year is roughly twice as likely to participate as someone earning less than $15,000.

Third serious mistake: not taking advantage of employers' contributions. Many employers match their workers' contributions, up to a certain amount. That is, if you contribute 3 percent of your salary to your 401(k) plan, your employer may match your contribution by adding an extra 1.5 percent to your 401(k) plan. That's a 50 percent return on some of your money. It's not just a free lunch. It's a free banquet. It's money in the bank, manna from heaven.

Yet many people don't even put the minimum amount of money into their 401(k) plans that would be matched by their employers!

Even people with both money and brains may foolishly ignore 401(k) plans. B. Douglas Bernheim, an economist, reported that Stanford University once began offering an "extraordinarily generous" plan under which the university contributed $2 for every dollar an employee put into the plan, up to 15 percent of the employee's earnings. "That's free money," he noted, "and nobody should turn that down. But an astonishing number of Stanford faculty—and these are well-informed, educated people—chose not to participate."

Of course, you may believe that you can't spare any of your salary, not even $100 or $500 a year—even though $500 a year is less than $10 a week. Still, as the saying goes, if you can't live on what you have, you cannot live on 5 percent less, either. So invest 5 percent.

There's no other investment you will ever encounter that may bless you so painlessly with a 50 percent or 100 percent return on your money. So beg or borrow (draw the line at stealing), but put at least enough money into your 401(k) plan so that your employer matches every cent you salt away.

Fourth bad mistake: not salting away more money. A survey sponsored by Merrill Lynch & Co. found that only about one-third of the participants contributed the maximum that they can (the maximum that's tax-deferred changes every year, in line with inflation). The *least* that you should contribute is the amount that's matched by your employer's own contribution.

Fifth mistake: not putting enough money into the stock market.

Yes, the stock market is scary. It's volatile; it can bounce up and down like a yo-yo. It can sink down and remain down for what seems like eternity. (See Key 22.) Yet, over the years, the stock market has rewarded investors more generously than fixed-income investments, cash equivalents (like money market funds), precious metals, antiques and collectibles, and so forth.

"To be investing almost exclusively in the safest asset available [guaranteed investment contracts]," Bernheim observes, "means that these people will get much lower returns than if their pension portfolio were professionally managed"—that is, if someone who knew what he or she was doing were managing the money.

Sixth mistake: putting too much money into your employer's stock.

Actually, the real mistake here is not being diversified enough—not having enough money in a basket of stocks.

Your employer may be a wonderful employer, fair and generous. The company may be a thriving enterprise, making money hand over fist. The stock may even be selling for less than it should.

It's still a bad idea to have one stock dominating your portfolio—even if you can buy the stock cheaply.

The stocks of great companies can take great falls. In 1999, even blue chips like Pfizer and Coca-Cola lost money.

How many stocks must you own to be fairly well diversified? The answer, according to one careful study, is twenty. With twenty stocks, if one stock falls off the table, you're not going to suffer the pains of hell. But even with twenty, there's a 10 percent chance that your portfolio will underperform the stock market (as represented by the Standard & Poor's 500 Stock Index) by 10 percent.

That study didn't consider that the twenty stocks might be in different industries, in which case you might not need so many as twenty. So let's say that you should own fifteen stocks in a variety of industries. What amount should any one stock compose of your portfolio? About 7 percent tops. So, by the same logic, your employer's stock shouldn't make up more than 7 percent of your investments. If it does, start cutting back.

Seventh mistake: not having a guide to how your money should be invested—an "asset allocation model."

How much should you have in stocks, in bonds, and in cash? The answer depends upon your age, your goals, your overall prosperity, your "risk tolerance." You should sit down and decide how your money should be divided, then roughly follow that model. (See Keys 40–44.)

Eighth mistake: investing too aggressively.

If you're approaching retirement, you probably shouldn't be 80 percent in the stock market—unless you don't need your 401(k) money to live on and you intend to leave it all to your children, your grandchildren, or someone else decidedly younger. Or unless you have so much money that you can live on just the stock dividends.

Who would choose to invest too aggressively? Perhaps people who don't know that between 1972 and 1974 the stock market, as represented by the Dow Jones Industrial Average, lost 48 percent of its value. And that if you had invested in a well-diversified basket of stocks in 1929, before the great crash, you wouldn't have received your money back for eight years.

Only the very bravest people, it has been said, should have as much as 80 percent of their investments in the stock market.

Ninth mistake: blindly following the leaders.

Let's say that stocks did fabulously in the past three months, fixed-income investments did woefully. So you shift your asset allocation, moving toward stocks and

4

away from bonds. The next three months, stocks go to heck in a handbasket and bonds soar to the skies. So you change your positions again. . . .

This is known as "market-timing," trying to avoid bear markets (when prices go down) and enjoy bull markets (when prices go up).

Market-timing has a foul reputation. One clever investor has said that if anyone could ever correctly divine whether stocks will be going up or down, he or she would own the world in three months—"one month with leverage." (*Leverage* means borrowing money to invest.)

Actually, market-timing can be successful. But practitioners who don't lose their shirts tend to make fairly modest shifts between stocks, bonds, and cash, not frequent and drastic changes. So, if you have an opportunity to invest in a market-timing fund with a good track record, consider it.

But don't market-time on your own. Most people should consider themselves long-term investors, ready to accept bear markets along with bull markets.

Tenth mistake: not rebalancing.

Let's say that you think you should be 60 percent in stocks, 40 percent in fixed-income investments. A few years elapse. The stock market does wonderfully, the bond market does frightfully. You're now 80 percent in stocks, 20 percent in bonds. You're probably too much exposed to the risk of the stock market at this point. Cut back on your stocks—and either add to your bonds or put money into cash equivalents, like money market funds. (See Key 26.)

Eleventh mistake: withdrawing money from your 401(k) plan when you don't have to. (See Key 51.)

Surveys have found that of the people who receive lump-sum distributions from their pension plans because of retirement or a job change, one-third spend all of it; the rest save some and spend some; only 11 percent roll the entire balance over into another retirement plan.

Twelfth and last mistake: overconfidence. It's probably a desirable quality in most areas of life, enabling us to apply for jobs we're not fully qualified for and to pursue tasks outside of our normal skills. But with the stock market, overconfidence leads people to trade too often and to take too many risks.

Paul Slovic, a professor of psychology at the University of Oregon, gave seventeen horse players information about forthcoming races. He found that the more information he gave the gamblers, the more confident they felt about who would win the races—but their accuracy actually didn't increase at all.

"The message is that feelings of confidence are not trustworthy," Slovic concluded.

In a famous study of 60,000 discount-brokerage accounts, Terrance Odean of the University of California-Davis found that overconfident investors traded too often, and that frequent trading was linked to poorer results. Said Odean, "The central message is that trading is hazardous to your wealth."

Harvard Financial Planners in Cambridge, Massachusetts, has come up with its own list of "ten common 401(k) mistakes."

1. Basing investment choices on the recommendations of coworkers. "One size does not fit all." Their needs and desires may not be the same as yours.
2. Choosing the seemingly safest investment, without recognizing that all investments involve risk and that, often, the more risk, the more reward.
3. Assuming that the most risky investment will automatically bless you with the greatest reward.
4. Buying everything. If the company offers ten funds, for example, putting 10 percent into each one. Many people do this. You may wind up with too much in stocks, too much in bonds, and a lot of duplication.
5. Putting most of your assets into company stock.

Some companies match only the investments you make in company stock, so sometimes it's unavoidable.

6. Not contributing to a 401(k) because you don't like the choices. If the company matches your contribution, you might choose an innocuous investment, like a guaranteed investment contract.

7. Not looking at your entire portfolio—your IRAs, for example, and your spouse's retirement plan—to make sure that your investments are well diversified.

8. Trying to time the market—moving from stocks to bonds or cash and vice versa. If you want to market-time, you're best off buying into a market-timing fund.

9. Taking the money when you leave your job and not keeping it in a retirement plan.

10. Not making sure that you invest enough so as to get the very highest match from your employer.

2

THE CASE FOR 401(K) PLANS

A 401(k) plan can shower you with blessings.

First off, the money you put in is not taxed (up to a yearly limit, $10,500 in 2000).

Your earnings are also not taxed—until you withdraw the money.

Your employer may even toss some money into your pot—perhaps 25 cents for every dollar you contribute, up to 7 percent of your salary (which might be $30,000). So, if you contribute $2,100, your employer may kick in $525. That's $2,100 multiplied by .25. And that's a 25 percent return on your money—which hasn't even started working for you!

When you add your employer's matching contributions and any after-tax deposits you make, the yearly limit is $30,000—or less if your plan sets its own limit on what you can contribute.

The highest amount of earnings that can be considered in determining how much you can put into your 401(k) is $170,000.

Generally, you can salt more away into a 401(k) plan than a deductible individual retirement account.

A chief advantage of 401(k) and most other retirement-savings vehicles is that you aren't taxed on the money you put away. Here's how much you might save in a tax-deferred investment as opposed to a taxable investment:

The Benefits of Tax-Deferment

	Tax-Deferred	Taxable
Year 1	$ 2,200	$ 2,200
Year 5	13,431	12,271
Year 10	35,062	29,400
Year 15	69,899	53,314
Year 20	126,005	86,697

Difference: $39,308.

This chart compares the growth of tax-deferred annual investments with similar taxable investments over twenty years. Assumptions: average annual total return of 10 percent, reinvestment of all dividends and capital gains, and a 31 percent tax bracket.

If you can show good reason, you may even borrow from your 401(k) plan—and even permanently withdraw some of your money before reaching age 59½ (the official age when you're able to withdraw your money without penalty). But your particular plan must authorize these transactions.

If those aren't enough incentives for you to invest in a 401(k) plan, here's another:

When you approach retirement, you may find that you need a lot more retirement money than you had suspected. Today's young people probably won't have it as good as the older generation.

- In the 1980s, the older generation benefited from rapidly rising house prices. Young homeowners may not enjoy the same property appreciation.
- "Because many of today's workers defer marriage and parenthood until well into their thirties or later, they may face all at once the expenses [that] families once [were able to] spread over several decades, making it harder to save for retirement," reports Mary H. Cooper in *CQ Researcher*.
- With the population growing older, the pool of young people paying for the Social Security benefits of older people is shrinking. The qualifying

age for Social Security recipients has been moved up; it may be moved up again. Social Security benefits of the well-to-do are now subject to taxes; in the future, those taxes may be even more severe.

- People are living longer—and spending more time in retirement.

- Many companies, especially small ones, are replacing their "defined benefit" retirement plans with plans that shift most of the financial burden to the employee, via "defined contribution" plans, like 401(k)s. With a defined contribution plan, the employee must decide whether to invest—and how much—and what to invest in. The dangers here are that (1) employees may choose not to take advantage of their 401(k) plans; and (2) they may invest their money in the plans too conservatively or (less likely) too aggressively.

One estimate is that 401(k) plans will provide about 50 percent of the retirement income for people retiring in the year 2012, compared with about 15 percent for current retirees.

All of which argues for people to be more generous than ever in saving for their retirements, and to start earlier.

Yet the evidence that Americans are doing the right thing isn't there.

People in their thirties and forties, warns B. Douglas Bernheim, an economics professor, must triple their rate of savings to avoid a sharp decline in their living standards when they retire.

There's evidence that Americans are hardly saving at all. In fact, a study commissioned by the Consumer Federation of America and Primerica found that half of American households have less than $1,000 in net financial assets.

Sources of Retirement Income

Here is where workers expect their retirement income to come from:

Employer pension/retirement plans:	28%
Social Security:	26%
Personal savings, life insurance, investments, other assets	16%
401(k) plans, thrift plans	14%
IRAs	10%
Tax-sheltered annuities	6%

Based on a survey of 1,000 full-time employed adults by Pulse Surveys of America.

3

WHAT THE TERMS MEAN

Both **401(k) plans and 403(b) plans** enable employees to save for their retirement and enjoy the benefit of having the money they put away go untaxed until they take it out.

They are called "defined contribution plans" because employees can squirrel away a certain (defined) amount of money each year. The amount that they can put into such a plan is the "contribution."

But 403(b) plans are open only to employees of public schools, churches, and certain tax-exempt organizations. These employees are not permitted to participate in 401(k) savings plans. (457 plans are for employees of federal, state, and local governments.)

Other key differences between 403(b) and 401(k) plans:

- Workers who take part in 403(b) plans are curently allowed to make larger annual contributions than people in 401(k) plans.
- Employees in 403(b) plans who accumulated money in their accounts before 1987 can delay receiving their distributions until they reach age 75. Employees in 401(k) plans must begin receiving their money by age 70½.
- People who receive distributions from 401(k) plans may be eligible for a reward when they take their money out: they may be able to take advantage of five-year or ten-year income averaging, which should lower their tax bite. This is not the case with distributions from 403(b) plans.

Equity means ownership. When you encounter the word, usually it means "stocks." An "equity" fund is a mutual fund composed of stocks. (You may also have heard the word in the phrase "home equity loan," a loan that uses your house as collateral. Here, "equity" means your free-and-clear ownership of the house.)

Stocks give you part ownership in a corporation. If you own ten shares of AT&T, for example, you are one of the owners of AT&T. Among other things, you are entitled to receive dividends—if the corporation is actually paying dividends. The prices of stocks typically bob up and down day after day, depending on what people are willing to buy or sell the shares for. If a company is prospering and raises its dividend, for example, the stock's price will probably go up. If the company is being savaged by the competition and it may have to cut or abolish its dividend, the price will probably go down.

If stocks are ownership, fixed-income investments (loosely called **bonds**) are "loanership." You just lend money to a corporation or a bank or an insurance company, and get regular interest. Interest differs from dividends in that dividends are more likely to change—to be raised or cut or abolished. On the other hand, bond prices are less likely to rise or fall as much as stock prices. If you pay $10,000 for a bond, you will receive only your $10,000 back at **maturity**—maybe in five, ten, twenty, or thirty years. Stocks don't mature. But there's no guarantee that you'll receive back whatever money you invested in a stock.

Mutual funds are investment companies that buy stocks or bonds or both. An equity mutual fund gives you a variety of stocks—along with someone (a manager) who decides what to buy and what to sell, what to pay and what to receive, and when. (Unless it's an index fund. See Key 31.)

With a fixed-income mutual fund, you can buy a variety of bonds—Treasury securities from the U.S. government, bonds from corporations that are thriving (investment-grade bonds), bonds from corporations under a cloud (junk or high-yield bonds), mortgage-backed securities, and so forth. Usually, you also get a manager who decides what to buy and what to sell, what to pay and what to receive, and when.

Money market funds buy short-term debt obligations. These funds are very safe but they won't normally make you much money. Money market funds keep their price per share fixed at $1, and if interest rates go up, they just lower their yields in order to maintain the share price at $1. (Another term for price per share is **net asset value**.)

Guaranteed investment contracts are like certificates of deposits you buy at banks—but you buy these from insurance companies. Like money market funds, they are very safe but they normally won't make you much money. (See Key 33.) In many plans, you cannot sell your GICs and move into other fixed-income investments, such as money market funds. This is to keep investors from selling GICs when interest rates on money market funds are rising.

Cash equivalents are any investment that can readily be turned into cash—without your losing much, if any, money. Any fixed-income investment that matures in less than a year is considered a cash equivalent. Examples: a one-year CD, money market funds, Treasury bills, one-year guaranteed investment contracts.

Asset allocation means how much you invest in stocks, bonds, and cash. A sort of all-purpose model: 50 percent in stocks, 40 percent in bonds, 10 percent in cash or cash equivalents.

Rebalancing means rejiggering your portfolio if your asset allocation goes out of whack. If you want to be 50 percent in stocks, but the market has soared and you're now 60 percent in stocks, you might cut back your stocks and move more money into fixed-income investments and cash equivalents.

Market-timing means trying to avoid **bear markets**

(when investment prices sink) and to enjoy **bull markets** (when prices climb). It is the Holy Grail of investing— desirable, difficult, and dangerous.

Dollar-cost averaging means investing regular amounts of money over regular periods of time. That way, you don't buy when the prices of whatever you're buying are unusually high, ripe for a fall. This applies to both stocks and bonds. If you regularly put money into a retirement plan, you're in effect practicing dollar-cost averaging.

Qualified means that contributions to a retirement plan are tax-deductible, and you don't pay taxes on the money. With an IRA, a $2,000 contribution may be subtracted from your taxable income. With a 401(k) plan, your contribution doesn't appear as income on your W-2 form. But you do pay Social Security taxes on 401(k) contributions, and one state (Pennsylvania) taxes 401(k) contributions. Some cities also tax the contributions.

Risk tolerance means how readily you can cope with volatility—and volatility means the ups and downs of an investment. Your risk tolerance obviously depends, to a large extent, on your investment experience and your sophistication.

A **portfolio** comprises all your investments—stocks, bonds, CDs, limited partnerships, whatever. You can have a tax-sheltered portfolio (IRAs, 401[k]s, Keoghs) and a taxable or private portfolio.

A **Certified Financial Planner** (CFP) is someone who has passed a test to give financial advice and has several years of experience. For the names of local CFPs, phone the Institute of Certified Financial Planners in Denver (800-282-7526). For planners who charge fees and aren't paid by commissions, phone the National Association of Personal Financial Advisors at (888) FEE-ONLY. Fee-only planners are usually the better choice.

4

VARIETIES OF RETIREMENT PLANS

Retirement plans generally let you postpone paying taxes on income that you sock away for your old age.

Some employer-sponsored tax-favored savings plans—like 401(k)s—are the new kids on the block. They differ from the older "defined benefit" plans in that most of the contributions are made by the employees themselves; the contributions are voluntary; and the employees must decide for themselves how the money is to be invested.

Employees can put away any amount up to a fixed percentage of their earnings. In other words, your contribution is *defined,* or spelled out. Most employers—92 percent of those with 401(k) plans—match these contributions with smaller amounts, up to a percentage (usually 6 percent) of an employee's salary.

With a defined-contribution plan, you aren't guaranteed the amount you will receive later on. The amount you receive will depend on how you invest your money—wisely or foolishly, aggressively or conservatively. With the older defined-benefit plan, your employer invested your money and promised that you would receive a certain amount. Your benefit (what you would receive) was defined.

Employees in defined-contribution plans typically have at least three choices of where to put their money: stocks, fixed-income investments (like guaranteed insurance contracts), and a combination of stocks and bonds (a "balanced" fund).

If your plan permits, you can borrow money from

your defined contribution plan before you reach age 59½. (After that age, there's no penalty.) You won't owe income taxes on the money you borrow, provided that you pay it back.

Other varieties of defined contribution plans, besides 401(k)s:

- 403(b) plans for employees of nonprofit, charitable, religious, or educational organizations.
- Section 457 plans for state and local government employees.
- Federal thrift savings plans for employees of the federal government.

Defined-benefit plans guarantee monthly benefits to employees. The employers decide how the pension money is to be invested, and they are responsible for investing the money prudently.

People who take part become "vested" (entitled to the benefits they have earned) typically after up to five years of work. The normal retirement age is 65, but employees can retire as early as age 55, depending on the plan, and receive 62 percent of the benefit they have earned. The size of the benefits usually depends on the number of years you have worked, along with your average earnings during the last years you work.

Keogh or **HR-10 plans** are for the self-employed, including freelancers who are covered by retirement plans from their employers. A "profit-sharing" Keogh allows you to defer paying taxes on 13 percent of your self-employment income, up to a $30,000 contribution a year. You must set up a Keogh plan before the end of the year for which you want to salt away retirement money, although you need not put in any money until April 15 of the following year.

Simplified Employee Pensions are similar to other defined-contribution plans, but without all the paperwork. You can set up a SEP in the same year you make a contribution. To participate, you don't necessarily have to be self-employed.

17

See the next Key for information on Individual
Retirement Accounts.

Schematic of How 401(k) Plans Work

Available	Employees of for-profit businesses
Best for	Everyone
Maximum contribution	Up to $10,500 in 2000
Tax breaks on contributions	Yes
Tax breaks on earnings	Yes
Company contributions	Varies, but usually up to 6% of salary
Fees	Usually 1%–1.5% of assets every year
Early withdrawals*	In cases of hardship
Investment options	Usually 11

*10% tax penalty on withdrawals before age 59.5 unless due to death or disability.

5

401(K) PLANS VS. TRADITIONAL IRAs

The Superiority of 401(k)s. 401(k) plans are typically much better than traditional Individual Retirement Accounts, and given a choice, you should spring for a 401(k) or 403(b) plan. Here are the reasons:

- Whereas the highest tax-deductible amount that you can salt away into an IRA in one year is $2,000 (or $2,250 for a spousal IRA), you may be able to put five times as much into a 401(k) plan—and even more into a 403(b) plan. The theoretical maximum for a 401(k) is $10,500 in 2000. (But the maximum may not be permitted if the plan discriminates in favor of highly paid employees, or if a complex rule, called Section 415, limits contributions.)
- Your employer may contribute to your 401(k) plan; many employers fork over 50 cents for your dollar, up to a limit (such as up to 6 percent of your salary).
- You may be able to borrow the money in your 401(k) plan—something that you cannot do with an IRA.
- In certain circumstances, you can withdraw the money from your 401(k) or 403(b) plan before age 59½. This would be the case if you withdraw the 401(k) money to pay certain medical expenses. To qualify, the expenses must be tax-deductible. That means that they must exceed 7.5 percent of your adjusted gross income. (Adjusted gross income is the amount on the last line of page one of Form 1040, the standard federal tax form.) Another case where you can withdraw 401(k) money early: if you're disabled.

- If you withdraw your 401(k) money in a lump sum (all at once) when you retire, you can use a special tax break called "forward averaging." This allows you to pay taxes on that money as if you had withdrawn it over the course of five years, rather than in just one year. That should lower the tax bite, simply because you may wind up in a lower tax bracket.

- One final benefit of a 401(k) plan: some mutual fund families that normally charge a load (sales charge) may drop the charge when people invest via a 401(k) plan.

Tax Aspects. People may think, erroneously, that there are important differences between the deductibility of a 401(k) plan and a deductible IRA.

Not so.

With a 401(k) plan, the money is automatically taken out of your paycheck to go into your retirement plan. The money that's removed isn't taxed (apart from Social Security taxes). The 401(k) money also isn't added to the income on the W-2 Form that you receive in January or February in the succeeding year.

With an IRA, on your tax return you declare the amount of the deduction (on line 24 of Form 1040) so that a corresponding amount of your taxable income escapes taxation.

Tax-wise, the major difference between 401(k)s and IRAs is that 401(k)s are a bit simpler to deal with. There's less paperwork. Things are done automatically.

The Case for IRAs. Traditional IRAs have advantages, too. Right now, you probably have a far wider variety of investment choices with IRAs. Certain 401(k) plans give you very limited choices.

Also, with IRAs you can move in and out of different investments very readily. If you make a trustee-to-trustee transfer (you instruct a brokerage firm or mutual fund, say, to handle the transaction directly), you can make as many changes as you wish—without paying income taxes plus the normal 10 percent IRS tax penalty. If you instruct the current custodian of your IRA to send the money to you, and you move it into a rollover IRA within 60 days, you also won't have to pay taxes and a 10 percent tax penalty. But you're limited to one tax-free rollover a year this way.

With a 401(k) plan, your ability to switch your investments may be limited. Some employers, for example, let you make changes only once every three months.

Only certain people can still deduct from their income all or part of their contributions to an IRA. Employees not covered by employer-sponsored retirement plans—or whose adjusted gross incomes are under certain amounts—can deduct up to $2,000 a year that they put into an IRA. Workers with higher earnings can take a percentage of the $2,000 deduction.

401(k)s Plus IRAs. In certain circumstances, you can have both a deductible IRA and a 401(k) plan. Normally, you cannot have a deductible IRA if you (or your spouse) has access to a company retirement plan, like a 401(k). An exception is when your adjusted gross income is under certain amounts.

Another instance where you can have a 401(k) plan as well as other retirement plans is when you have income from self-employment. With the freelance income, you can set up an HR-10 (Keogh) plan or a Simplified Employee Pension plan.

When IRAs Are Deductible

Year	Maximum Income for Singles	Gross Income for Couples Filing Jointly
2000	33,000	53,000
2001	34,000	54,000
2002	35,000	55,000
2003	40,000	60,000
2004	45,000	65,000
2005	50,000	70,000
2006	50,000	75,000
2007	50,000	80,000

6

401(K) PLANS VS. ROTH IRAs

No alternate investment is as good as a 401(k) plan that matches your contributions to any significant extent. Not even a Roth IRA, even though a Roth IRA may permit you to withdraw your money and not owe any taxes on the appreciation of your assets. This makes the Roth IRA more desirable than a traditional IRA, at least for young people.

Besides, a Roth IRA, unlike a traditional IRA, doesn't require any minimum distributions after you reach age 70½. You can withdraw your principal at any time without tax or penalty. An exception to this is when you transfer the assets from a traditional IRA: You must then wait five years to escape a tax or penalties.

Contributions to a Roth IRA aren't tax deductible, but if you have had the account for five years or more and you are 59½ or older, the assets you withdraw aren't subject to federal income taxes. With a traditional IRA, contributions are tax deductible, but the assets you withdraw will be taxed.

Single people with adjusted gross incomes of up to $95,000 and married people with adjusted gross incomes of up to $150,000 can contribute $2,000 a year to a Roth IRA. Taxpayers with adjusted gross incomes of $100,000 or less may convert all or part of a traditional IRA to a Roth IRA, but must pay taxes on the original tax-deductible contribution plus any growth. The $100,000 includes the amount scheduled to be converted.

Another advantage that a 401(k) plan has over a Roth IRA is that you can contribute more than $2,000 a year.

If you can invest in both a 401(k) plan and a Roth IRA, it's a good idea to invest more aggressively in the Roth IRA because any gains may never be taxed.

7

HOW TYPICAL IS YOUR 401(K) PLAN?

Some 36.7 million people now have 401(k) plans, and the average balance recently was $75,000.

The average 401(k) plan matches 68 cents on the dollar, according to a survey by the Spectrem Group, and 92 percent of all plans do have some sort of match.

More than 90 percent of employers allow investors to borrow half of their 401(k) accounts, up to $50,000.

The typical plan now offers investors around 11 choices, though there are reports that foreign funds are still not very common. Typical choices include large-company stock funds, small-company stock funds, company stock, balanced funds (half stocks, half bonds), index funds, guaranteed investment contracts, fixed-income funds, and money market funds.

A very desirable addition to the 401(k) lineup are life-cycle funds, which allow an investor to purchase an entire portfolio of stocks and bonds, suitable for his or her age and goals, via one simple investment.

Another welcome change is that more employers are arranging for their 401(k) investors to get personalized, detailed advice, sometimes via local financial planners and sometimes via an outside service, like the online services FinancialEngines and 401KForum. (See Key 54.)

On the other hand, many employers are still timid about giving advice, fearing lawsuits later on if their advice doesn't work out.

Some 10 percent of plans now give investors a brokerage "window," so they can buy almost any stock or mutual fund they could possibly want. While this option is wonderful for sophisticated investors, the brokerage fees may be high, and so much freedom to trade may overwhelm inexperienced investors.

Thanks to State Street Brokerage Services in Boston, employees of Pepsico and other companies can choose among more than 1,200 mutual funds—along with any number of individual stocks and bonds.

To discourage investors from gambling rather than investing, State Street urges individuals to invest no more than half their plan assets in a brokerage account. Still, one officer says that "We assume people who use brokers are astute." Most of them, in fact, prefer mutual funds to individual stocks.

8

HOW GOOD IS YOUR 401(K) PLAN?

A simple way to evaluate your plan is to ask: How much does your company match of every dollar you contribute? And at what point does the matching stop?

Three Key Numbers. It's easy to get confused by the key numbers in 401(k) plans.

First: *What amount can you contribute to a 401(k) plan?* Your employer might set a limit of 10 percent of your salary. So, if you're earning $30,000, you can contribute up to $3,000.

Next: *What does your company match of every dollar you contribute?* 25 cents? 50 cents? A dollar? More? Let's say that it's 75 cents. So, if you contribute $1,000, your employer would contribute $750—75 cents on the dollar.

Finally: *Up to what percentage of your salary would your employer match?* Let's say that it's 5 percent. Your salary is $30,000, so your employer would match up to $1,500 (5% times $30,000). That means you would receive a maximum of $1,150 (75% of $1,500) if you contributed at least $1,500.

Here's the formula:

Maximum you might receive = company match per $1 you contribute × percentage of salary your company matches (. . . provided that this is less than the percentage of your salary that you are allowed to contribute that will be tax-deferred).

Another way to judge a 401(k) plan: *Does it have a good variety of choices?* Three choices are common: stocks, guaranteed investment contracts, and money market funds. Eleven is also fairly common, and might include a fixed-income fund and a balanced fund.

Beyond stocks, GICs (see Key 33), a fixed-income fund, and balanced funds, you might want an index fund for stocks, an index fund for bonds, a fund that invests in foreign stocks, a fund that invests in foreign bonds, a fund that invests in small U.S. companies, and various types of fixed-income funds (investment grade corporate bonds, low-rated bonds, mortgage-back securities).

A fairly new option is an asset-allocation or a life-cycle fund, which does it all—one-stop shopping. This is a sensible choice for employers to offer to unsophisticated investors. (See Key 34.)

IBM offers a Balanced Asset Fund, a sort of "fund of funds." It combines five other IBM funds offered to employees: 40 percent in an index of large companies (like the Standard & Poor's 500 Stock Index), 30 percent in a fixed-income fund, and 10 percent each in a small-company index fund, an international stock fund, and a U.S. government securities fund. IBM recommends the fund, which has 60 percent in stocks, to people in the middle of their careers.

With your own 401(k) plan, check how each fund has performed in the past—if it's not a new fund. Or see if you can find the portfolio manager's track record. Go to a library and inspect *Morningstar Mutual Funds* or *Value Line Mutual Funds*, both of which are newsletters, or issues of *Business Week, Money*, or *Forbes* that rate mutual funds.

In evaluating any funds, stress the three- and five-year records, but look at the one-year and ten-year records, too.

Another way to evaluate 401(k) plans: *Do the employers give their workers guidance?* Some companies provide newsletters, seminars, lectures, and even suggested asset-allocation models (how much you should have in stocks, bonds, and cash, depending on your age, prosperity, and goals).

IBM employees can figure out how much to con-

27

tribute by using a computer program that considers their salary, possible investment returns, possible inflation rates, expected Social Security benefits, and even income from their spouses' pension plans.

Some employers allow their workers to change their allocations every day; others permit it only four times a year. No one wants to encourage workers to switch in and out—that's only for daring, sophisticated investors. On the other hand, being able to switch only every four months would be frustrating if the stock market began declining steadily on bad economic news, or if interest rates started climbing as inflation seemed to be roaring back.

By the same token, there's a dispute over how often assets inside 401(k) plans should be valued. Monthly? Daily? The trend is toward daily.

There's no easy conclusion, but erring on the side of greater freedom usually seems to be the better idea.

In short, the most desirable 401(k) plans have

- generous employer matching contributions, both as to the dollar amount matched per dollar of worker contribution and to the limit;
- a healthy variety of choices, including foreign stocks and bonds and an asset-allocation fund;
- money managers—and funds—with good track records;
- a worker's ability to switch investments more than once every quarter; and
- company-sponsored guidance, via newsletters or lectures.

A quick way to evaluate your plan has been issued by HR Investment Consultants in Baltimore, and published in *Newsweek*. (The very last item seems like a criticism of defined-benefit plans, where the employer is responsible for the investments.)

Who pays?

Grade: A

You pay for investment management, your boss pays for administration.

Grade: C

You split administrative fees.

Grade: F

You pay for everything.

Investment fees

Grade: A

Program offers some funds with low annual expense ratios, like 0.2 percent for index funds or bond funds.

Grade: C

Expense ratios in the 1 percent range.

Grade: F

Fund expenses over 1.25 percent, along with extra charges.

Info. & advice

Grade: A

A financial adviser helps you choose your funds.

Grade: C

Asset-allocation information and portfolio planning software, inhouse or online.

Grade: F

"Didn't we give you that booklet last year? Here, watch the video again."

The match

Grade: A

Employer matches first 3 percent of your salary, it's 3 percent whether you contribute or not, or matches more than 3 percent.

Grade: C

50 percent on the first 6 percent.

Grade: F

No match.

Loans

Grade: A

"You have a phone, you have a loan."

Grade: C

Limited borrowing, formal application needed.

Grade: F

Hardship withdrawals only.

Vesting

Grade: A

Immediate.

Grade: C

Five years for full investing, at 20 percent a year.

Grade: F

More than five years.

Investment choices

Grade: A

A brokerage account, eight fund choices, two or three life-cycle funds.

Grade: C

One fund family, eight funds.

Grade: F

Employer does the investing.

9

THE PERFECT 401(K) PLAN

Just because a 401(k) plan gives you a generous matching contribution doesn't mean that it's the best.

What if the choices of investments are few, and ill-chosen at that? What if you can invest only in the stock of your employer, and your employer is a fading old-line company? Or if your employer requires that you work five years before you get vested, five years before you can join up? And you can't borrow any money—or even withdraw any money if you're about to be evicted?

In short, you must evaluate a 401(k) plan on a variety of touchstones, not just one.

Still, the matching contribution, if not all-important, is very important indeed.

There's one company that matches its employees' 401(k) contributions $4 for every $1. Up to 5 percent of their salaries. So, if you earn $50,000 or more, and salt away up to $2,500 (5% of $50,000), this company will invest $10,000 in your name.

The source of this information is Ted Benna, the gentlemen who pioneered 401(k) plans. But he won't reveal the name of the company because he's sworn to secrecy. (I suspect that it's a pharmaceutical company.)

On the subject of the perfect 401(k) plan, Benna had this to say:

- A good match is $1 for $1, up to 6 percent of your salary. Typical is 50 cents on the dollar, up to 6 percent.
- As for the total that you can contribute, the IRA rule is 25 percent of your pay. (This 25 percent

limit includes your contribution and your employer's contribution.) A maximum of $10,500 of that, in 2000, is tax deferred. An ideal 401(k) lets you salt away the maximum, which might be 19 percent if your employer matches 6 percent, or 20 percent if the employer matches 5 percent, or 25 percent if your employer matches nothing.

- How long must you wait before you can contribute? Some companies let you contribute from day one, some have a 90-day waiting period.
- When do you get vested—entitled to all the money the company has contributed for you? Benna thinks the answer is immediately. Others accept a 90-day waiting period. Some companies require five years.

What about investment choices? *Worth* magazine proposes three sets of offerings:

1. Three to five funds that invest in an asset-allocation model suitable for the age and goals of the particular investor. In other words, "life-cycle" funds. (See Key 34.)
2. Five to ten core investment offerings, letting hands-on investors customize their asset allocations.
3. Two dozen additional offerings, at least, plus a "window" to a brokerage account or to a mutual fund supermarket, where you can buy a variety of funds.

All the offerings, *Worth* adds, should rank in the top quarter or one-third of their peer groups over three to five years, with low fees to boot.

Other nice things: the ability to trade every day. (Dangerous for amateurs but demanded by the sophisticated.) Daily access to your fund's performance, which is compared to benchmarks like indexes.

Also, lots of educational literature and lectures—or, as Benna puts it, "A high degree of handholding." Even, perhaps, an outside impartial expert to advise you about your choices and to monitor your portfolio—ideally, paid by your employer.

Your employer should also be willing to let you borrow money for any reason at all under God's heaven. (This definitely encourages people to invest.)

One final desideratum: the company listens to its employees. One autocratic employer I once worked for haughtily ignored everyone's suggestions—including my own proposal, years ago, that it offer an index fund based on the Standard & Poor's 500.

10

WHAT BIG COMPANIES OFFER

A generous 401(k) plan isn't the only thing to look for in a retirement plan if you're scouting around for a new job or comparing your benefits with those of other companies.

Procter & Gamble, for example, doesn't even offer a traditional pension plan to its employees. Still, it will give up to 25 percent of pay to a tax-deferred account for its employees, based on their years of service. The average contribution is 15 percent. That's remarkably generous, even without a 401(k).

Money magazine surveyed a variety of giant U.S. companies on their benefits. Here's a look at what some of these companies offer just in the way of 401(k) plans. (Companies listed higher up were judged to have better benefits overall.)

Xerox: no match.

Dell Computer: matches 100 percent on employee contributions up to 3 percent of their earnings.

Chevron: matches 100 percent on employee contributions up to 2 percent of their earnings.

Bellsouth: matches employee contributions up to 6 percent of their earnings.

Duke Energy: matches employee contributions up to 6 percent of their earnings.

Allstate: matches 150 percent of employee contributions, up to 5 percent of their earnings.

Ford Motor: matches 60 percent in stock on 10 percent of their earnings.

Freddie Mac: matches 50 percent to 100 percent up to

6 percent of their earnings, depending on years of service.

General Motors: matches 70 percent on up to 6 percent of their earnings.

AT&T: matches 67 percent on up to 6 percent of their earnings.

Bank One: matches 100 percent on 6 percent of pay after seven years.

American Express: matches 100 percent on up to 3 percent of their earnings. Employees can contribute 15 percent of their earnings.

GTE: matches 75 percent on up to 6 percent of pay.

Aetna: matches 100 percent on up to 5 percent of their earnings.

Johnson & Johnson: matches 75 percent on up to 6 percent of their earnings.

Target: matches 100 percent on up to 5 percent of their earnings.

General Electric: matches 50 percent on up to 7 percent of their pay. Employees can contribute 15 percent of earnings.

Raytheon: matches 100 percent on up to 4 percent of their earnings. Employees can contribute up to 20 percent of their pay.

IBM: matches 50 percent on up to 6 percent of their pay.

Metropolitan Life: matches 133 percent on up to 3 percent of their earnings. Employees can contribute up to 16 percent of salary.

Du Pont: matches 50 percent on up to 6 percent of their pay.

Sprint: average 401(k) matches 66 percent on up to 6 percent of their earnings.

United Parcel Service: matches 100 percent on up to 3 percent of their earnings.

Cardinal Health: matches at least 50 percent on up to 6 percent of their earnings.

Lucent Technologies: matches at least 50 percent on

up to 6 percent of their earnings.

Chase Manhattan: matches 100 percent on up to 5 percent of their earnings.

New York Life: matches 100 percent on up to 3 percent of their earnings.

Electronic Data Systems: matches 25 percent on up to 6 percent of their earnings. Employees can contribute more than 16 percent of their earnings.

Merrill Lynch: matches 50 percent on up to 4 percent of their pay. Employees can contribute 15 percent of their pay.

American Airlines: no match.

Ingram Micro: matches 50 percent to 100 percent, based on years of service, on up to 5 percent of their pay.

UnitedHealth Group: matches 50 percent on up to 6 percent of their earnings.

Columbia/HCA: matches 25 percent on up to 6 percent of their earnings.

K Mart: matches 50 percent on up to 6 percent of their earnings. Employees can contribute 16 percent of their pay.

McKesson HBOC: matches 50 percent on up to 6 percent of their pay. Employees can contribute 16 percent of their earnings.

11

THE DOWNSIDE OF
401(K) PLANS

There's a case against 401(k) plans: ordinary investors may not know how to invest in them properly. They may do dumb things—including not investing in them in the first place. They may invest in them so unwisely that they wind up losing money, either directly or just to inflation.

A 401(k) plan requires that you take charge of your own investments, and that means—unfortunately—that some unlucky people are going to be blown out of the water.

A survey by John Hancock Financial Services has found that almost half of 401(k) participants thought that money market funds contained stocks and bonds.

Only 25 percent knew that the best time to buy bonds is when interest rates are declining. (When rates decline, existing bonds are worth more.)

The critics don't argue that employees should avoid investing in 401(k) plans altogether. They argue that employees must be encouraged to learn more about them—through reading whatever literature a company may provide or reading books like this one.

At one time, employees didn't have to invest voluntarily; they didn't have to manage their own money. Defined-benefit plans ruled the roost. Now these traditional plans are being replaced by defined-contribution plans, particularly among small companies. And John Doe and Jane Roe must now make vital investment decisions on their own.

The basic questions are: 1. Do enough people opt to

make 401(k) contributions? 2. Do they invest enough? 3. Do they invest wisely?

The answers are not encouraging.

"If you look at people with under $25,000, the percentage participating is very low," reports Cindy Hounsell, director of the Women's Pension Project at the Pension Rights Center in Washington.

A survey, by Hewitt Associates, found that while most 401(k) plans permit employees to put away up to 15 percent of their income, the employees on average contributed 5 percent to 8 percent.

CQ Researcher quotes a middle-manager at a large corporation as saying, "Many of my company's employees have entry-level jobs, limited proficiency in English, and minimal education. I have no idea how a person holding a $5-an-hour job is supposed to make those kinds of [investment] decisions."

An Education Department study, mentioned by Professor Bernheim, showed that, among people aged 21 to 25, only 44 percent of whites, 20 percent of Hispanics, and 8 percent of blacks could accurately determine how much change they were owed from the purchase of a restaurant meal consisting of two items.

Concludes Bernheim: "It therefore seems highly improbable that most individuals have mastered more advanced concepts such as compound interest, risk-return tradeoffs, inflation adjustments. . . . Most individuals have at best a primitive understanding of the relations between their financial choices and economic outcomes; they are poorly equipped to evaluate economic opportunities and vulnerabilities."

Summing up, Bernheim says: "We have this peculiar situation now. To a greater and greater extent, people are placing the responsibility for saving on their employers by relying primarily on their pensions and Social Security rather than on personal saving. At the same time, the employers are pushing the responsibility back to them by saying, 'You guys have got to make more decisions.' But those are decisions that workers are not prepared to make, and no one's telling them how. In the end, no one takes responsibility, and the investment decisions are made poorly."

What Investors Want. A survey, by J. P. Morgan, found that employees may not be so unsophisticated as some skeptics believe. Here's what they wanted in a 401(k) plan:

- balanced funds (stocks and bonds) as an investment option
- bond funds and not just GICs
- active management rather than passive (an index fund is passive)
- frequent valuation of their assets

One discouraging note: They liked company stock.

The Woman Question. In saving for retirement, women may have a harder time than men. They live longer, so they need more retirement money. Of American women born in 1950 who will reach age 65, the average age at death is expected to be 87; of American men born in 1950 who live past 65, the average age at death is expected to be 81.

More than half the women who live past 65 are expected to spend time in a nursing home, which will exhaust the savings of many of them.

Besides, women earn less than men—about 76 cents to the dollar. So they have less to put away for their retirements. And because many of them take off time to raise children, they work fewer years than men, thus lowering their future Social Security and pension benefits.

Further, women tend to work in small firms, without unions, firms that are less likely to provide retirement benefits.

Beyond all that, a Merrill Lynch survey has found that fewer women than men had started saving for retirement at ages 30 or 40. One reason: They may not be as financially sophisticated.

Perhaps because they are less likely to hold financial positions, twice as many women (35 percent) as men (17 percent) in the baby-boom generation said they felt uninformed about their retirement benefits. And more women than men in general said that they would rather have someone else manage their retirement money.

In short, women especially need guidance—to start early, to save consistently.

To keep people from making costly investment mistakes, employers should give them more guidance.

- They should provide a regular newsletter about properly investing in 401(k) plans and sponsor seminars as well. Bernheim suggests that employers be given more protection against lawsuits from unhappy employee-investors in return for providing investment advice.
- They should provide asset allocation models— based on a worker's age, prosperity, financial sophistication, and needs.
- For people who desperately need guidance, employers should give simple, good advice, such as:

If you're not sure how to invest your money, put it in a balanced fund, a life-cycle fund, or guaranteed investment contracts.

Try to put 10 percent of your income away; at least put away whatever amount your company will match.

It is not smart not to take advantage of your company's free contribution.

12

WHAT PEOPLE ACTUALLY DO

A survey of 7.9 million active participants in 401(k) plans conducted by the Employee Benefits Research Institute and the Investment Company Institute found that

- 49.8 percent of the average portfolio was in stock funds;
- 17.7 percent of the portfolio was in company stock;
- 8.4 percent was in balanced funds (stocks and bonds);
- 11.4 percent was in guaranteed investment contracts;
- 4.7 percent was in money market funds; and
- 0.3 percent was in stable value funds, similar to GICs.

If you add the stock funds to the company stock and to half the balanced funds, you get 71.7 percent—suggesting that the average 401(k) investor has two-thirds of his portfolio in stocks. The percentage may be even higher now, in view of the continuing bull market. A more recent, more limited survey found that 76 percent of investors' 401(k) assets were in the stock market.

Not long ago, many observers were worried that the average investor had too little in the stock market. Now there's concern that some investors have too much in the market and may panic when the market takes a steep decline, as it will inevitably.

Even so, many financial planners continue to report that too many investors are still avoiding stocks and glomming on to GICs and other fixed-income investments. That's why some studies have found a sharp difference between the results of 401(k) investors at the same companies—some have emphasized stocks, others bonds.

There's also concern that so many people invest in the stock of their employer, thus putting their investments and their jobs in one basket. Hewitt Associates has reported that in 401(k) plans where company stock is a choice, one-third of the average investor's assets are in that stock—"the ultimate nondiversification disaster," one financial planner has called it.

Other findings: younger investors were more exposed to stocks than older investors, as you would expect. People in their twenties had 62.1 percent of their 401(k)s in stocks. People in their sixties had 39.8 percent in stocks.

In plans that offered company stock, the amount that investors had in stock funds was lower. If GICs were offered, investments in bonds and money market were lower.

Some 30.6 percent of the investors had no money in stock funds—but more than half owned company stock or balanced funds. So they really had 38.5 percent in the stock market.

Still, some 20 percent had no money in stocks at all. Of course, they may have owned stocks outside of their 401(k) plans—in other retirement vehicles or in their private portfolio.

More than 60 percent of job changers withdrew their money instead of keeping it with the old plan, rolling it over to an IRA, or transferring it to a new employer's 401(k).

At any one time, 23 percent of investors had loans against their accounts. More than half of the companies let their employees have more than one loan outstanding.

13

TYPES OF 401(K) INVESTORS

Fidelity Investments surveyed 700 investors with 401(k) plans that Fidelity handled. The company broke them down into eight investor types, based on three life-stages:

People Between 35 and 50. "Concerned but harried" types made up 50 percent of these midlife people, who compose 65 percent of all 401(k) investors. Only 35 percent of these people contribute the maximum to their 401(k)s; as many as 50 percent have taken out loans. No wonder they're harried! Not surprisingly, 39 percent rate themselves as beginning investors.

They're worried about their retirement and worried about their debt loads. Their average account balance is $46,692.

"Confident planners" make up 25 percent of these midlife investors. They have an average balance of $92,860, nearly double that of their "concerned but harried" peers. Some 48 percent contribute the maximum to their 401(k) plans, and only 19 percent have taken out loans. Half make their own investment decisions, and 40 percent rate themselves as experienced. They invest 91 percent of their assets in the stock market—very confident indeed.

"Uninvolved savers" rate themselves as beginners and prefer to spend as little time as possible making investment decisions.

People Over 50. "Relaxed achievers" make up 45 percent of this group, and they have an average account balance of $194,507. Most contribute the maximum, and only 22 percent have taken out loans. They're very experienced investors. They spend one to six hours a month on financial planning, and most do further research.

"Preretirees in need" resemble "uninvolved savers." They consider themselves beginners and don't want to spend any time with investment decisions.

People Under 35. "Eager beginners" are the biggest group here, and 26 percent are contributing the maximums to their 401(k)s. Some 34 percent have taken loans from their accounts. Average balance: $15,132. They're very much involved with financial planning and monitoring their own accounts.

Also in this group are "less-involved beginners" and "serious self-starters."

The most worrisome thing about these profiles, says Fidelity's Kathryn Hopkins, is the prevalence of loans. Loans may help out with family needs, she points out, but investors lose the power of compounding when they borrow their own assets.

Loans, in many cases, are making significant reductions to the amount of wealth that investors can accumulate for their retirement.

Who borrows the most? Those between 35 and 50—"concerned and harried." Who borrows the least? "Relaxed achievers," at 22 percent. No doubt the people between 35 and 50 have an excuse. They are buying houses and putting their kids through school.

14

WHY YOU SHOULD
START YOUNG

Tom, Dick, and Harry decided to put money into retirement plans. Tom started putting $1,440 into a tax-deferred annuity at age 40, and continued every year.

An annuity is an investment that's tax deferred but may not give you a tax deduction. Annuities are like nondeductible Individual Retirement Accounts, but—unlike IRAs—you can contribute an unlimited amount. You buy annuities from insurance companies, and usually can choose stocks, bonds, or both. An annuity in which contributions are tax deductible is called a "qualified" annuity. Tom's annuity was not qualified.

The amount that Tom invested every year was $1,440—which would have been $2,000 except that he had to pay taxes on the $2,000 at a rate of 28 percent. ($2,000 × .28 = $560; $2,000 − $560 = $1,440.) He directed his money into diversified investments in the annuity, and received an 8 percent yearly total return.

When he reached age 65, Tom had $124,435 in his annuity.

Dick also invested $2,000 a year, and the $2,000 was pre-tax because it was in his 401(k) plan. So he actually invested $2,000 every year, not $1,440.

He, too, started his investment program in his forties, and he too invested in a diversified portfolio that blessed him with an 8 percent yearly return.

What was different was that Dick's employer matched half of his contribution, to the tune of $1,000 a year, which is common with 401(k) plans.

Thanks to his investing all of the $2,000 and to his

employer contributions, when Dick reached 65 he had amassed $259,052. Twice as much as Tom.

True, Tom didn't have to pay taxes when he withdrew his contributions—because they had already been taxed. (He would still owe taxes on the appreciation.) Even so, despite owing taxes Dick came out far ahead.

Harry also invested $2,000 a year into a pre-tax and tax-deferred pension. He, too, received 8 percent a year. And he, too, benefited from his employer's 50 percent match, receiving $1,000 extra.

But Harry started ten years earlier. At age 30 instead of age 40.

When Harry reached the age of 65, he had $606,211 in his pension plan.

That's 234 percent more than Dick.

And 487 percent more than Tom.

(These calculations come from Merrill Lynch & Co., Inc.)

Lessons:

- It pays to invest in a pre-tax and tax-deferred vehicle—a pension plan like a 401(k) rather than just a tax-deferred vehicle, such as an annuity or nondeductible IRA.
- It pays to take advantage of your employer's generosity in putting money into your pension plan.
- It pays to begin putting money into your pension plan early.

Here's another instance of how valuable it can be to start investing early.

If John Doe puts $2,000 a year into a pension from age 19 to 25, then stops, he will have $1,035,160 at the age of 65 (assuming that the money compounded at a rate of 10 percent a year).

If Jane Roe puts $2,000 a year into a pension beginning about when John Doe stopped, at age 27, and stops at age 65, Jane Roe will wind up with only $883,185.

Yet John Doe invested only when he was 19, 20, 21,

22, 23, 24, and 25. A total of only seven years.

And Jane Roe invested when she was 27, 28, 29, 30, 31, 32, 33, 34, 35, 36, 37, 38, 39, 40, 41, 42, 43, 44, 45, 46, 47, 48, 49, 50, 51, 52, 53, 54, 55, 56, 57, 58, 59, 60, 61, 62, 63, and 64. A total of 38 years—5.2 times as long as John.

And yet John wound up $151,975 ahead.

To repeat the lesson: Start early.

By starting early, you will have the option of retiring earlier. Or retiring at a normal age and living more luxuriously.

And if you're ever out of work for a long time—because of losing your job or because of illness—you'll still be well on the way to a comfortable retirement, even if you skip saving for a few years.

Should you ever need the money you put away, for an emergency, you can probably borrow it.

Finally, if your employer matches your 401(k) contribution to any extent, go for it—no matter what your age. It is just plain foolish to turn down an opportunity to get free money.

15

HOW MUCH TO CONTRIBUTE

You should, first of all, contribute to your 401(k) plan an amount up to the point where your employer matches your contributions. Whether the limit is 3 percent of your salary or 6 percent of your salary, go for it.

You would be losing the opportunity to earn up to 100 percent on some of your money.

Let's say that your employer matches your contribution dollar for dollar up to 2 percent of your salary. Your salary is $30,000. If you salted away $600 a year, that means that your employer would give you another $600. In other words, in one year you would double your money.

If you're short on cash and feel that you need every last penny you earn, you could borrow money. Borrow from friends, relatives, from any whole-life insurance policies you have. Get a home equity loan. Get a personal loan.

Even if you hate going into debt, consider: Whatever rate of interest you pay on the money you're borrowing, it will not be close to even 25 percent.

There is no rational excuse to skip contributing to a 401(k) plan up to the amount that your employer matches.

Ideally, you should contribute the maximum—even beyond whatever percentage is matched. In many companies, you can contribute 15 percent of your salary.

But there are two provisos:

- First, you need insurance coverage against what otherwise might be financial catastrophes—life insurance (if someone depends on your income), health and disability insurance (if you don't have sufficient coverage from your office), homeowners or renters insurance (which also gives you liability insurance—in case someone sues you, for instance), automobile insurance, and insurance if there's ever a judgment against you over $100,000 (umbrella insurance).

- You should have an emergency fund—roughly equal to 10 percent of your yearly salary, or three to six months' income. It's mainly to protect you in case you or your spouse lose your job, but it's also there for other emergencies: you might owe the IRS more than you thought, for example, or you or a family member might lose a lawsuit.

Once you have enough insurance, and the right kind, along with an emergency fund, put as much money as you can spare from your other goals (buying a house, starting a business) into a retirement plan. Key 16 provides a guide to how much money you will need each year to afford a comfortable retirement.

Most people don't sock enough away into their retirement plans.

But keep in mind that you can contribute too much. Years ago, according to *Medical Economics* magazine, one physician had contributed the maximum to his defined benefit Keogh plan all of his working life. At the age of 72, when he retired, he discovered that he had $72,000 a month coming in from his retirement plans— $864,000 a year. His children were well-to-do; he himself was not a big spender. He finally realized the error of his ways: he should have spent more money on himself and his family before retiring—by taking more vacations, for example.

It's better, of course, to err on the side of having too much money in retirement than too little. Still, estimate how much money you can put into a retirement plan without having to make painful sacrifices in your personal life. Eating out only once every two weeks as opposed to every week is no big sacrifice, nor is keeping your old furniture another year. But not going on a vacation this year may be too much of a sacrifice; postponing visits to physicians is even more undesirable and unwise.

If you have access to a 401(k) plan and you could put more money away, consider not funding a traditional IRA or SEP (if you have the right to). A 401(k) is better than most other retirement plans, so very likely you should forget about funding other plans. An exception might be for a Roth IRA, if you're young, or a Keogh plan, if you have a lot of freelance income: you can salt a lot of money away into a Keogh plan, and you can avail yourself of a special form of income averaging when it comes time to withdraw your money.

By the same token, you may be saving in other ways—such as by reinvesting your distributions from stocks or stock funds and bond funds. You might stop such reinvestments, to have more money to contribute to your 401(k) plan.

Reinvesting your money into stocks or bonds does help you practice a rough form of dollar-cost averaging. (See Key 45.) And such reinvestments build up your personal portfolio, which you can get access to easily—not always the case with money in a 401(k) plan. But if you have 10 percent of your yearly salary available for emergency money, you can safely leave your personal portfolio alone—and let it appreciate only by means of capital gains, not reinvested distributions. (That means that you should rely on a stock's climbing from, say, $10 to $15 a share, rather than from the reinvestment of any dividends.)

Exception: if you own a stock that lets you reinvest your dividends at a discount, *and* you have confidence in that stock, *and* it doesn't constitute too large a part of your portfolio, you might continue reinvesting your dividends—as opposed to putting more in your 401(k) plan.

But, for most people, it's unlikely that a stock that allows dividends to be reinvested at a discount is part of a diversified portfolio. Financial experts think you need

50

about fifteen stocks in about ten industries to have a truly diversified portfolio—one that probably won't badly underperform the stock market.

What about selling assets in your private portfolio, so as to have more money to live on, and thus more of your salary to put into a tax-deferred, diversified retirement plan?

It depends on your circumstances. Keep in mind that you need some liquidity—some ready money to deal with emergencies, to take advantage of investment opportunities. So don't put all of your eggs in one basket, even if the basket seems as safe and sturdy as a 401(k) plan.

Besides, your 401(k) plan may not offer you enough options. If it doesn't have foreign stocks and foreign bonds, or small-company U.S. stocks, you should consider investing in such desirable areas on your own—via your personal portfolio or via another retirement plan that you have access to.

Finally, remember that you can correct mistakes. You can cut back on the percentage of your salary that you put into your 401(k) plan—or put more in.

16

HOW MUCH YOU WILL NEED

In 1935, when 65 became the official retirement age in this country, the average life expectancy was 77 years. Today it's about 85. And people can expect to spend as much as 25 percent of their lives in retirement. So it's wise to plan on your living for two decades after you retire.

For an estimate of your Social Security income, call 1-800-772-1213 to request a copy of your Personal Earnings and Benefit Estimate Statement (Form SSA 7004). Check your earnings on record every three years to confirm the accuracy of the information.

Here's when you will be eligible for full Social Security benefits:

Year of birth	Age
before 1938	65
1938	65, 2 months
1939	65, 4 months
1940	65, 6 months
1941	65, 8 months
1942	65, 10 months
1943–54	66
1955	66, 2 months
1956	66, 4 months
1957	66, 6 months
1958	66, 8 months
1959	66, 10 months
1960 and later	67

The longer you can wait to apply for Social Security, the more income you will receive.

As for how much you will need, researchers at th Georgia State University Center for Risk Management and Insurance Research, along with Alexander & Alexander Consulting Group in Atlanta, have come up with this table, which shows what percentage of your retirement income will come from savings and what portion will come from Social Security.

The higher your income, the greater the percentage of preretirement pay you'll need in retirement—in part because you'll still be paying high taxes.

The figures are for couples with one worker and no dependents. The figures for singles and for married couples with two workers would be somewhat lower up and down the line.

Preretirement Income	% Needed in Retirement	% Replaced by Social Security	% Needed from Other Sources
$20,000	76%	64%	12%
30,000	72	55	17
40,000	71	44	27
50,000	74	37	37
60,000	74	31	43
70,000	77	27	50
80,000	84	23	61
90,000	86	21	65
150,000	86	13	75
200,000	87	9	78
250,000	89	8	81

The following worksheet on how much you should save comes from Fidelity Investments:

How will you meet your retirement needs?	Example	Yourself
A. In today's dollars, enter your expected annual retirement expenses—use 60% to 80% of current income.	$50,000	_____
B. Subtract the total amount you expect to receive in retirement each year from your retirement plans.	$30,000	_____
C. Amount you will need annually in retirement from your personal savings (line A minus line B).	$20,000	_____

What is your retirement savings goal?

D. What is your target retirement age?
Choose the age and enter the number (factor)
from the table below.　　　　18.8　　　_____

Retirement age	55	60	62	65	67	70
Factor	21.5	19.6	18.8	17.4	16.4	14.9

E. Amount you may need to have saved by
your target retirement age
(line C times line D).　　　　$376,000　　　_____

F. If your target retirement age is younger
than 65, select the age and enter the number
from the table below.　　　　2.8　　　_____

Early retirement age	55	60	62
Number	8.5	4.6	2.8

G. Additional amount you may need to have saved
to provide additional retirement income until
Social Security and pensions begin, or to offset
reduction in these benefits due to early
retirement (line B times line F).　　　　$84,000　　　_____

H. Estimate total savings needed by your desired
retirement age (line E plus line G).　　　　$460,000　　　_____

What will your current savings be worth?

I. Amount you have saved, including retirement
plans and other savings.　　　　$50,000　　　_____

J. How many years do you have until you retire?
Enter the number from the table below.　　　2.7　　　_____

Years until retirement	5	10	15	20	25	30
Years number	1.2	1.5	1.8	2.2	2.7	3.2

K. Estimated value of your current savings at
the time you retire (line I times line J).　　$135,000

How do you achieve your retirement savings goal?
L. The amount you still need in addition to
your current savings (line H minus line K).　$325,000
M. Enter the factor from the table below for the
number of years until you retire.　　　　　.024

Years until retirement	5	10	15	20
Years factor	.184	.083	.050	.034

N. Amount you may need to save each year to
reach your goal (line L times line M).　　$7,800　_____

Assumptions: Your investments will yield 8 percent a year before retirement and 7 percent during retirement. Inflation will average 4 percent a year, and your spending will increase every year. You will live to age 90, longer than your statistical life expectancy. The primary goal of these savings is to provide retirement income, not to provide an estate. (That is, you may not have much left over.)

"Since all amounts are in today's dollars," states Fidelity, "you should actually increase your savings each year by the rate of inflation."

The example used is of a 37-year-old who plans to retire at 62.

17

401(K)s VS. PRIVATE PORTFOLIO

Most people probably don't have a sizable nonretirement (private or personal) portfolio. Virtually all of their investments are in their retirement plans.

But if you do have both, you must decide whether you will invest in them differently.

Here are some arguments for investing your 401(k) money and other pension assets more conservatively than your nonretirement portfolio:

- You enjoy relatively low capital-gains taxes on money in your private portfolio. The current top bracket for long-term capital-gains taxes is 20 percent. But you won't enjoy low capital-gains taxes on money coming out of your 401(k) plan. You could be taxed as high as 39 percent, just on the federal level. True, only on large sums of money would there be a big difference between the returns of money in a private portfolio and a retirement plan. But large amounts of money may indeed be involved. "It may pay some investors to reserve qualified retirement plans for taxable fixed-income investments," counsels Standard & Poor's *The Outlook*, "thus deferring taxes on investments that would be subject to substantially higher ordinary-income rates outside the account." Still, *The Outlook* continues, "you may find that the potential return from well-chosen stocks is so much greater than that of fixed-income investments it compensates for the tax differential. A popular alternative is to balance 401(k) or IRA accounts with stocks and bonds."

- You can deduct losses you have in your nonretirement portfolio. If a stock or a mutual fund goes down, you can sell it for a tax loss, using the proceeds to buy a more promising investment or—if you have confidence in the original investment—switch to something similar. This can be financially rewarding and psychologically comforting.
- Typically you will have more choices of different types of stock investments outside of your 401(k) plan. Not all 401(k) plans offer their employees enough choices. Besides, there are advantages to investing outside one family of mutual funds: you get subtly different—or drastically different—investment styles.
- Typically you can make changes faster with investments outside of a 401(k) plan. While this is a two-edged sword, it is certainly helpful to sophisticated investors, those who make major moves only in the face of overwhelming evidence—selling stocks, for example, when the stock market clearly becomes overvalued. In 1987, sophisticated investors with money in certain pension plans were anguished that they couldn't switch out of stocks when they saw the crash coming.
- If you might need your retirement money—you're disabled, for example, and have large medical bills—you want most of your money there when you need it. You don't want to lose half of your stock-market investment, which is what happened in 1972–1974, and have to wait until 1979 to break even. You don't want to have to wait for the stock market or the bond market to revive. In other words, you don't want to lose your rainy-day money in a freak storm.
- You might more readily panic if your retirement money takes a hit—and you might sell in a temporarily bad market. Whereas slow, steady gains in a retirement portfolio may make you relaxed, even

if—in your private portfolio—you're losing money to a bear market. There is something worse than the mistake of not having enough invested in the stock market in your retirement account. And that's having enough invested in the stock market in your retirement account, but selling out in panic near the bottom of a bear market.

In short, there is a good case for investing your private money more aggressively than your 401(k) money The case for stocks in a 401(k):

- If most of your investment money is in retirement plans like the 401(k), as is true of many people, your putting the money into the stock market is almost unavoidable. Otherwise, you might not have enough money invested in the stock market.
- Research by Morningstar suggests that if you have ten years or fewer to invest, putting fixed-income funds into tax-deferred accounts seems to be better. Between ten and twenty-five years, it is a standoff. But if your horizon is more than twenty-five years, you're better off putting your stocks in retirement accounts. The stocks benefit enormously from the compounded growth of reinvested short-term capital-gains distributions.

Overall, the best answer seems to be to spread your bets. It's not a given that the next five, ten, or twenty-five years will be the same as the last five, ten, and twenty-five years, and that stocks will be the investment of choice for retirement plans. As a general rule, put conservative stocks or conservative mutual funds into your retirement accounts. But consider diversifying with some fixed-income funds and small-company funds as well.

One area of agreement seems to be that the investments in a Roth IRA should be the most daring—like small-company stocks, which over the long run have performed even better than large-company stocks. The idea is that because a Roth IRA shields its assets from taxes, you want the highest possible return.

A study by James B. Wiggins of Michigan State University concluded that allocating assets with higher expected returns (stocks) to a Roth IRA and assets with lower expected returns (bonds or cash) elsewhere produces the highest expected retirement wealth.

But you don't want to gamble with a Roth IRA, especially if it's a big component of your retirement savings. If you want to invest aggressively, you might choose a volatile mutual fund with a good long-term record—not do something so adventuresome as invest in individual small-company stocks on your own. And if you are going to invest daringly with a Roth IRA, you would be wise to invest more conservatively in your 401(k) plan and other retirement accounts.

18

WHAT TO INVEST IN

Over the years, stocks produce the greatest profits by far of any investment. Far better than gold, far better than antiques and collectibles, far better than money-market funds, far better than fixed-income investments in general. The stock market is where the big money is.

In 1926, if you had invested $1,000 in U.S. Treasury bills, $1,000 in long-term government bonds, $1,000 in big-company common stocks, this is how you would have fared by the end of 1998:

Asset	72-Year Annual Return	After Inflation
Treasury bills	3.9%	0.8%
Long-term bonds	5.7	2.6
Common stocks	11.2	8.1

The message is that almost all investors should have a goodly percentage of their assets in the stock market.

If you look at how the assets inside typical 401(k) plans may fare in the future, the argument in favor of stocks becomes even more compelling.

This chart assumes that someone invests $1,000 a year for thirty years in various investment options. A GIC is issued by an insurance company, and resembles a certificate of deposit. (See Key 33.)

Five Investment Choices/Rates of Return	Lump Sum at Retirement	Annual Income for 25 Years
Stock mutual fund (10% annual return)	$164,494	$15,000
Stock mutual fund/guaranteed investment contract	110,289	10,300
Government securities fund (7% return)	94,461	8,850
Government securities fund/GIC	75,262	7,050
Guaranteed insurance contract (4% return)	56,085	5,250

Unfortunately, this comparison of investment options is very iffy. The rates of return are certainly not guaranteed. It is, for example, unusual for a government securities fund to do so well as to return 7 percent a year. In an inflationary period, government securities might perform poorly.

Still, the message of this chart is clear: stocks, or some combination of stocks and fixed-income investments, usually do best.

The mixed portfolios in the chart, like the second one on the list (stock fund plus GIC), are presumably never rebalanced back to their original fifty-fifty split. That's why they return more than 7 percent, which would be the average return of a combination of a stock mutual fund (10 percent) and a guaranteed investment contract (4 percent)—and what a government securities fund would have returned.

Stocks, it must be said, are also volatile. And people who cannot remain on the roller coaster without getting motion sickness should limit their exposure to stocks. In the past the market has taken such vicious losses that eight years were needed before those losses were recouped.

How much of your money you should have invested in stocks depends on your risk tolerance. (See Key 19.)

Some speculative investments don't belong in a 401(k) plan, and they are forbidden to be placed in such plans. Among them:

- options
- futures
- commodities
- limited partnerships
- individual holdings of precious metals
- individual holdings of foreign securities

Despite the last, through brokerage accounts in some 401(k) plans, investors can buy American depository receipts, representing foreign stocks traded on the New York Stock Exchange.

19

RISK TOLERANCE

Your "risk tolerance"—your ability to withstand a short or long stock-market decline without panicking and selling out—depends upon your psychological makeup, but also upon such things as

- your age. If you're young, you can assume more investment risk, normally, than later on during your life. You learn from your financial errors, and later you may profit by avoiding those errors. And you'll have time to make up the losses. If at age 22 you toss $2,000 down the drain buying an over-the-counter stock that your cousin Charlie recommended, it's better than throwing $2,000 down the drain thanks to cousin Charles when you're 62.
- your prosperity. If you have virtually no slack in your budget and a sudden expense might blow you away, you can be less risk-tolerant. When the rich are short of cash, they can keep one of their cars for another year instead of buying a new one, or not vacation on the Left Bank next month. The not-so-rich might have to sell stocks just when the market is down. Unexpected expenses might mean an IRS tax penalty or a lawsuit because your dog bit someone; or your car may need a transmission, your house may need a new roof.
- your investment sophistication. Smart investors welcome downturns in the market—if the downturns are apparently going to be short. Stocks become bargains, and it's a good time to increase your exposure to the market. These investors know in their bones and in their gut that the market,

despite its flightiness and sheer perversity, has always bounced back.

Unsophisticated investors become nervous whenever the market retreats; they rejoice when the market climbs. They buy when sophisticated investors sell, sell when sophisticated investors start buying.

One is not condemned to remain an amateur forever. Many investors, as they grow older, plow more money into the stock market—because they've become more knowledgeable. Using dollar-cost averaging, they buy no-load mutual funds with good long-term track records, intending to hang on through thick and thin—and especially through thin.

As they grow older, they may also become less timid about investing in general.

Your own risk tolerance should guide your investment decisions, in particular how you allocate your assets—how much you put into stocks, bonds, and cash. Obviously, the younger you are, the more prosperous, the more sophisticated, and the more courageous, the greater the percentage of your assets you should have invested in the stock market.

Here's a test that may guide you toward a suitable asset-allocation model. Add up the numbers that you circle in response to the seven questions.

	Strongly Agree	Agree	Neutral	Disagree	Strongly Disagree
1. Earning a high long-term return that will allow my capital to grow faster than the inflation rate is one of my most important investment objectives.	5	4	3	2	1
2. I would like an investment that provides me with an opportunity to defer taxation of capital gains and/or interest to future years.	5	4	3	2	1

	Strongly Agree	Agree	Neutral	Disagree	Strongly Disagree
3. I do not require a high level of current income from my investments.	5	4	3	2	1
4. My major investment goals are relatively long-term.	5	4	3	2	1
5. I am willing to tolerate sharp up and down swings in the return on my invest-ments to seek a potentially higher return than would normally be expected from more stable investments.	5	4	3	2	1
6. I am willing to risk a short-term loss in return for a potentially higher long-run rate of return.	5	4	3	2	1
7. I am financially able to accept a low level of liquidity in my investment portfolio. [Liquid: easy to turn into cash.]	5	4	3	2	1

Portfolio allocation models:

Total Score	Money Market	Fixed Income	Equities
30–35	10%	10%	80%
22–29	20	20	60
14–21	30	30	40
7–13	40	40	20

Copyright © William G. Droms

While you may be unwilling to accept these asset allocation suggestions, you may want to classify yourself according to your answers.

30–35	Very risk-tolerant
22–29	Above average in risk-tolerance
14–21	Inclined toward conservatism
7–13	Very conservative

20

THE IMPORTANCE OF DIVERSIFICATION

Ask stockbrokers how many stocks someone should own, and they may tell you half a dozen. After all, it gets devilishly difficult for the ordinary person to try to follow more than six stocks.

But academic studies have shown that you need fifteen or twenty stocks to protect yourself from the risk of your portfolio's doing much worse than the stock market (as represented by the Standard & Poor's 500 Stock Index).

During one year, according to John K. Ford, associate professor at the University of Maine, the average return on the 1,528 stocks listed on the New York Stock Exchange was 19 percent. (The return includes capital gains along with dividends.)

But there was a lot of variation among those stocks.

- 1% returned –60% or less.
- 1% returned between –50% and –60%.
- 1% returned between –40% and –50%.
- 1% returned between –30% and –40%.
- 3% returned between –20% and –30%.
- 5% returned between –10% and –20%.
- 11% returned between 0 and –10%.

In short, 23 percent of all the stocks returned from zero to minus 60 percent or less. That means 351 stocks.
To continue:

- 16% returned between 0 and 10%.
- 21% returned between 10% and 20%.
- 14% returned between 20% and 30%.

So the majority of the stocks, 51 percent, achieved returns between 0 and 30 percent. That's about 780. To proceed:

- 9% returned between 30% and 40%.
- 6% returned between 40% and 50%.
- 4% returned between 50% and 60%.
- 2% returned between 60% and 70%.
- 2% returned between 70% and 80%.
- 1% returned between 80% and 90%.
- 1% returned between 90% and 100%.
- 1% returned over 100%.

In short, 26 percent did wonderfully well, blessing investors with returns over 30 percent.

The point is that even when the stock market does well, and 26 percent of the stocks do splendidly, you can be unlucky. You might have owned only stocks among the 23 percent that lost money or just broke even. If you had owned just one stock, you had a 23 percent chance of having a bad year. And you might have lost over 60 percent of your money.

That's why you should diversify: own a basketful of stocks. You'll dilute the damage done by one or two or half-a-dozen clinkers.

The conventional wisdom is that you need fifteen to twenty stocks so as to track closely what the Standard & Poor's 500 does.

But Professor Ford's study found that even if you owned twenty different stocks,

- there was a 10 percent chance that your portfolio would have underperformed the market by 10 percent or more;
- there was a 26 percent chance that your twenty-stock portfolio would have lagged the market by 5 percent or more; and
- there was a 40 percent chance that your twenty-stock portfolio would have lagged the market by 2 percent or more.

"Clearly," Professor Ford concludes, "there is a substantial amount of risk that can be avoided by diversifying beyond 20 stocks."

How many stocks must you own to be pretty sure of not lagging behind the market by not more than 2 percent? You would have a 30 percent chance of missing the market by only 2 percent if you own at least ninety stocks. In other words, if you don't want to risk doing much worse than the market, diversify among lots of stocks. Ford's conclusion: "investing in a large number of stocks is necessary to approximate the performance of the market with some reasonable degree of confidence."

No one is recommending that you own ninety different stocks. Fifteen or twenty stocks in various industries would probably do—if you could afford the commissions, if you could follow them carefully, if you're an astute and sophisticated investor. (Ford did not consider how many stocks you would need if you bought stocks in different industries. If one industry falters, most of the stocks in that industry would suffer, too.)

Ford's recommendation, though, is the sensible one: "The results make a strong case for investing in common-stock mutual funds that are diversified. . . ." Mutual funds may own 50 to 100 to 500 stocks, thus giving you the diversification you need.

Diversification means spreading the risks by buying an entire smorgasbord, not just the appetizer or the dessert. After all, if you had been lucky in 1988 you could have invested in one of the fifteen stocks that blessed you with total returns over 100 percent. Or you could have been unlucky and invested in one of the fifteen stocks that cursed you with total returns of –60 percent or less. By spreading your bets, you won't be blessed or cursed. That's the point of diversification: avoiding the extremes. The opposite of diversification is gambling.

You should diversify not just among the stocks you own. You should also diversify the *kinds* of stocks you own: foreign and domestic, large company, midsized company, and small company. You should diversify by *investment styles*, buying the stocks of growing companies, the stocks of undervalued companies, and the stocks of companies paying high dividends.

Diversify your fixed-income investments, too. Buy not just Treasury bills, which come due in a year or less; also consider buying notes (two to ten years) and bonds (ten to thirty years), so you're diversified by *maturities*. This is known as "laddering," and you can do it with CDs, corporate bonds, and municipal bonds, too. If you have a choice in your 401(k) plan, don't just stick with one-year guaranteed investment contracts; buy other types of fixed-income investments, and with longer maturities. (But be wary of long-term fixed-income obligations. Most investors would do better sticking with short-term or medium-term bonds.)

A more useful way to evaluate the volatility of fixed-income investments is called "duration"; that calculation takes into consideration when the investments provide interest. The more frequently, the lower the risk.

Try to diversify your fixed-income investments not just by their maturities (or durations) but by their types: Treasuries, high-grade and high-yield corporates, mortgage-backed securities, foreign bonds.

Diversification has one danger: It may become what Peter Lynch, former manager of Fidelity Magellan, has called "diworsification." Don't buy undesirable investments just to be better diversified. Commodities in general, for example, are not suitable for the vast majority of investors. Fortunately, you cannot buy certain questionable investments for a retirement plan: commodities, precious metals, paintings, and so forth.

But if your 401(k) plan does offer a variety of stock or fixed-income mutual funds, do nibble on many of them—foreign stocks along with domestic stocks, Treasuries along with corporate bonds.

And don't have much of your 401(k) money in your company's stock. If fifteen or twenty stocks may give ou adequate diversification, it follows that you shouldn't have more than 5 percent to 7 percent of your portfolio in company stock.

21

STOCKS

The stock market is where the big money is. It is also where big money is lost.

In fact, the claim has been made that more people lose money in the stock market than make money in the market. Evidence comes from accountants, financial planners, and stockbrokers, who report that their new clients (in the case of planners and brokers) are always holding many more losers than winners.

Stocks—common stocks, as opposed to preferred stocks, which are more like bonds—give you part ownership in a corporation. Big-company stocks tend to be traded on the New York Stock Exchange. Midsized company stocks, on the American Stock Exchange. The most popular small-company stocks are in the NASDAQ electronic system, but the NASDAQ has large companies, too—like Microsoft.

Stocks may bless you with dividends and capital gains. Capital gains represent the appreciation in a stock's price. If a $100-a-share stock pays $5 in dividends in a year, and its price goes up to $110, its appreciation is $15, or 15 percent—$5 in yield, $10 in appreciation. ($15/$100 = 15 percent.)

Types of Stocks. Among the various types of stocks:

- blue chips, the stocks of old-line companies, which typically pay rather high dividends but aren't growing at a very fast clip. The stocks in the Dow Jones Industrial Average are blue chips: ExxonMobil, AT&T, IBM, General Motors, and so forth.
- cyclical stocks, which do well when the economy

is bouncing along, but poorly when the economy falters. Example: auto stocks.

- growth stocks, those of companies that are making more money year after year. Recent examples: Microsoft, Cisco, and Qualcomm.
- defensive stocks, those of companies that seem to do well no matter what the economy brings— beverage companies, for example. People don't cut back on their beer-drinking in bad times.
- income stocks, companies that aren't growing very much but that pay high dividends. They aren't necessarily as financially healthy as blue chips. Example: utilities.

A good way to differentiate between types of stocks is to look at their price-earnings ratios, listed in newspapers. The P/E ratio (also called the multiple) gives you an idea of what investors are willing to pay for a stock. The price alone is almost meaningless. But when you take the earnings into account, you have a good clue as to how popular a stock is.

Blue chips and income stocks tend to have low price-earnings ratios. They aren't growing very fast.

Growth stocks may have very high price-earnings ratios.

Cyclical companies may also have high P/E ratios. The reason is that their earnings may have faltered—but their prices have remained relatively high.

Stocks are also segregated into small company, mid-sized, and large company. The way company size is measured is to multiply the price by the number of shares outstanding. The result is called market capitalization.

Why People Lose Money. Why do so many people lose money in stocks—when stocks generally are the single most profitable investment?

- People extrapolate. When individual stocks or the stock market as a whole go up, investors conclude that the market is going to continue going up.

(Actually, individual stocks and the entire market may have become overpriced, ready for a plunge.) Or when individual stocks or the market retreat, investors may conclude that they should sell before the market goes down even more. (Actually, the market may be underpriced then, ready for a rise.) But by extrapolating—assuming that the number that comes after 1, 3, 5, and 7 is 9—people lose money by buying high and selling low.

- Extrapolation wouldn't be so harmful if the market were stable. But the stock market and most stocks are giddily volatile. If stock prices went like this: 2, 3, 3, 4, 3, 5, 6, 6, 7, . . . , extrapolation wouldn't be such a threat. But stock prices tend to make big leaps and suffer big declines, like this: 2, 1, –4, –5, 3, –1, 6, ...

True, over the years the stock market eventually trades higher, despite the wild roller coaster ride. But many people jump out of the rollercoaster way before it begins to hug the ground.

- People don't own enough stocks. The typical investor may have five or six. That means that if one or two stocks plummet, the investor may be out a lot of money. And some stocks do poorly for reasons that were unpredictable. A promising new medical product, for example, may have disastrous side-effects—which no one could have forecast. Even if an investor has the number of stocks he or she should have—fifteen or twenty, in various industries—that person probably wouldn't have the time to study all of them, and perhaps to sell those of companies that are faltering.
- Ordinary investors don't have fresh information. They don't have analysts who spend their time talking with top management, testing the product, talking with competitors, talking with suppliers, and reading the trade magazines. The analysts'

information doesn't go directly from them to you. It goes directly from them to the big players—like the managers of gargantuan mutual funds, who have billions of dollars to throw around.

There's a simple antidote to help keep people from losing money in the stock market: mutual funds. With mutual funds, you typically get a well-diversified portfolio, consisting of perhaps 100 stocks; you get a portfolio manager who buys when stocks are cheap and sells when stocks are expensive; you get a manager who has access to the fresh information that you and I get six months later, when the stock's price has probably climbed to the sky and has now become overpriced—or when the stock's price is now deep down in the basement.

22

BEAR MARKETS

The biggest danger of investing in stocks is not that there will be a bear market—a sharp decline in the value of most stocks.

The biggest danger is that there will be a bear market—and that you will panic and sell your shares. So, when the market eventually revives—when there's a bull market—you won't be there to enjoy the party.

Bear markets come with the territory. And they can be brutal. The market goes down faster than it goes up, and after a year of patiently waiting for your stocks to appreciate, suddenly—there go all your profits. And then some. If you've been planning to retire soon and you maintained a large exposure to stocks, you may wind up retiring a little later than you had expected.

How badly might a bear market maul you? In 1973–1974, the stock market—as represented by the Dow Jones Industrial Average—lost 48 percent of its value.

Even good investors began to despair. One man recalls that "It was like Chinese water torture. You thought that the market had bottomed, that it couldn't possibly go down any more. But it would go down more. Day after day." It took until mid-1980 for people to recover their losses from 1973: seven years.

Then came 1979, and *Business Week*—in despair—published one of the most famous cover stories in the history of magazine journalism: "The Death of Equities."

The 1980s, as it happened, witnessed one of the most glorious bull markets in history.

The good news is that bear markets are followed by bull markets. Bull markets last an average of 3.75

years—and gain an average of 117 percent from bottom to top.

The lesson is: If you are caught in a bear market, hang on. Gradually buy more stocks while they're selling for bargain prices.

To keep from panicking, don't keep too much of your worldly assets in stocks—especially if you're within five years or so of retirement. It may take you 5.2 years to get your money back—if not longer.

The lesson is not that you shouldn't invest in the stock market. The lesson is that you expect a bear market—and be prepared to ride it out.

A good way to protect yourself against bear markets, of course, is to own some of this and some of that—not just this or that.

Take stocks. U.S. stocks, foreign stocks, value stocks, growth stocks, big-cap stocks, and small-cap stocks don't march to the same drummer. If one asset class takes a nosedive, another may do OK—if not better than OK.

The same is true of bonds. Treasury securities, corporate high-grade bonds, junk bonds, mortgages, and foreign bonds may go in different directions.

Adding a little cash to a portfolio will also help protect you in times of trouble.

In general, of course, the more that your portfolio is tilted toward stocks, the more grievously wounded it will be during a bear market—as this chart, from Vanguard Group, shows.

Asset Allocation	Worst Loss (1926-1998)	Years with Losses (1926-1998)	Average Return
100% stocks	–43.1%	20 of 73	11.2%
80% stocks, 20% bonds	–34.9	19 of 73	10.4
60% stocks, 40% bonds	–26.6	17 of 73	9.4
50% stocks, 50% bonds	–22.5	16 of 73	8.9
40% stocks, 60% bonds	–18.4	16 of 73	8.3
20% stocks, 80% bonds	–10.1	12 of 73	7.1
10% stocks, 10% cash, 80% bonds	–6.7	9 of 73	6.2

23

COMPANY STOCK

You're fond of your company. It's been good to you—lending you money, paying you when you've been disabled, being supportive when you've had personal problems. You think the world of your management. The company's stock, everyone raves about. Low price-earnings ratio, healthy cash flow, low percentage of debt to equity, good return on equity, low price to book, everything checks out.

Should you put your entire 401(k) investment in company stock?

The answer is no. NO. *No.* **No!**

There's an investment cliché: A stock doesn't know that you own it. A stock is not a sentient, conscious creature. It is an investment.

Yet there are people who won't sell Columbia Gas or AT&T because their Aunt Tillie left the shares to them. And there are people so loyal to their employers that they wouldn't dream of doing anything so ungrateful and treacherous as selling their company's stock.

But it is not ingratitude to sell any company's stock. It can be suicidal not to.

Every stock can get overpriced—especially everyone's favorites. In 1999, even blue-chip stocks such as Pfizer, Coca-Cola, and Walt Disney went down.

The trouble with having a great deal of money in one stock is that your portfolio would not be diversified. If the company got into trouble, your portfolio could sustain enormous losses. If an investor needs a portfolio of fifteen different stocks to be properly diversified, no one stock should constitute more than 7 percent of his or her portfolio. (100%/15 = 6.66% of your portfolio.) Once you reach 7 percent, cut back.

Some employers tempt their workers to invest in company stock. They sell their shares at a discount. Or, in their 401(k) plans, the matching contributions they make are only to contributions to purchase company stock.

Those are incentives, all right. And you should certainly go for it—up to the point where employee contributions are matched. But with one proviso: The stock must be worth buying.

Go to a large library and check the stock in *The Value Line Investment Survey*, which rates about 1,700 stocks on their timeliness and on their safety. 1, 1 is best; 5, 5 is worst; 3, 3 is average. If your company's stock is rated below 3 for timeliness or safety, it's probably sensible for you to hold off buying any shares. *The Value Line Investment Survey* has an excellent record in forecasting stock performance.

Also, see how the stock is rated by Standard & Poor's *The Outlook*, a newsletter. Whereas *Value Line* stresses how well a company is doing, *The Outlook* also looks for undervalued stocks—those that haven't been doing well, but whose prices have fallen so far that they are now worth buying. *The Outlook*'s ratings are the opposite of *Value Line*'s: 5 stars is best. If a stock is rated 4 by *Value Line* for timeliness, but 2 by *The Outlook*, it may be worth buying. *The Outlook* also gives stocks a "quality ranking," similar to *Value Line*'s safety rating. Check that out, too.

In short: Buy your company's stock only if it's worth buying. And even if it's worth buying, don't let it dominate your portfolio.

24

FIXED-INCOME VEHICLES

Bonds—more precisely, fixed-income investments—used to be so safe and stable that they were boring. Not anymore. These days, interest rate changes—or the likelihood of such changes—can knock bonds down or drive them up with breathtaking speed.

You lend a corporation, a bank, an insurance company, a municipality, or the federal government some money; in return, the borrower pays you regular payments (called interest) for the use of your money (your principal). Upon an agreed-upon date (the maturity), you get your principal back. Whereas stocks are "ownership," bonds are "loanership."

Treasury securities have three maturities: up to a year (bills); two years to ten years (notes); ten years or longer (bonds). Strictly speaking, then, "bonds" mature in over ten years.

When interest rates in general go up, the value of existing bonds declines. When interest rates decline, the values of existing bonds go up.

Interest Rates	Bond Prices
rise	decline
decline	rise

There's a possible exception: the prices of junk or high-yielding bonds may rise when interest rates rise. Reason: Coming out of a recession, interest rates might rise a little as the economy strengthens—an indication that companies not doing well may prosper, and so might their bonds.

The major threat to any "bond" is inflation. When interest rates go up, the value of most existing bonds sinks like a stone.

Here's why: You buy a bond for $10,000, paying 5 percent interest. Then interest rates go to 6 percent. No one wants to buy your bond for $10,000. People may want to buy your bond for less than $10,000 because it pays less than the going interest rate. They might offer to pay $8,333.33 so they'll get 6 percent interest. (A $10,000 bond you buy for $8,333, paying 5% interest, will give you $500 a year. $500 is 6% of $8,333.) Actually, they would pay more than $8,333—because they would get $10,000 back at maturity, not just $8,333.

The longer the maturity of a fixed-income investment, the riskier it is. That's because, over a longer period of time, the issue may get into trouble. And you may have to sell the bond just when interest rates are unusually high—and your bond is worth less. It's because the longer the maturity, the greater the risk, that the further out you go into the future with a bond, generally the higher the interest rate.

Long = Risky. Bonds that won't be paid off for many years (with long maturities) get hit the most if interest rates rise—and make the most if interest rates fall. This chart assumes that interest rates rise or fall by 1 percent on bonds earning 8 percent a year.

Maturity (years)	Interest rates fall 1%, prices rise by ...	Rates rise 1%, prices fall by ...
1	1.0%	1.0%
5	4.2	4.0
10	7.1	6.5
30	12.5	10.3

To deal with interest-rate risk, you could stick with money market funds. Such funds are the safest fixed-income investments. Your interest may change every week, but your original investment remains stable. In effect, money market mutual funds are very short-term bonds. (See Key 26.)

Another way to deal with interest-rate risk is to concentrate on short-term bonds—those that come due in an average of less than five years. Then, if interest rates rise, you won't get badly hurt. Your interest can quickly buy higher-pay bonds.

You could also buy intermediate-term bonds instead— the "bullet" approach. That way, you would capture some of the higher yield of long bonds, but not suffer so much loss of principal if interest rates rose. An alternate way of doing this is to buy short-term and long-term bonds—the "barbell" approach.

If you think that long-term bonds are paying a lot and that interest rates will be coming down, naturally you would think of buying long bonds. But there's a saying among fixed-income investors: "long and wrong." For most individual investors, long bonds are too dangerous to justify the extra interest they usually pay.

When You'll Need Money

If you will need money in:	Consider
a few months	a money market fund
1 to 5 years	a short-term bond fund
5 to 10 years	intermediate bond fund
over 10 years	a long-term bond fund

Along with interest-rate risk, there's credit risk. The borrower may go out of business, or at least not be able to pay you 100 cents for every dollar you borrowed. Treasury obligations are the safest investment in the world: they are backed by the United States Government. Most municipal bonds are fairly safe to very safe. But some corporate bonds aren't: they're issued by shaky corporations. Naturally, these bonds pay unusually high interest. They have two names: high-yield bonds and junk bonds. Generally, high-yield bonds do well in times of economic prosperity or when people expect such prosperity, and fewer companies default on their obligations. In bad economic times, high-yield bonds do poorly because more companies default on their obligations.

For the average investor, high-yield bonds can be worth the risk if the investor has a variety of such bonds inside a mutual fund portfolio—and a portfolio manager and analysts who have decided which bonds are under-valued (their rewards are worth more than their risks). In any case, junk bonds should not constitute a large part of any typical investor's portfolio.

Risk vs. Reward

Type of Fund	Income Potential	Credit Risk
U.S. Government Securities	Lowest	Low
Investment Grade Corporate Bonds	Higher	Moderate
Junk or High-Yield Bonds	Highest	High

In evaluating a mutual fund of bonds, find out what the average credit rating is. Junk bonds get Standard & Poor's ratings of "BB" or lower, and "Ba" or lower from Moody's.

Fixed-income investments carry other kinds of risks, too. With mortgage-backed securities, for example, a key risk is prepayment: when interest rates go down, people holding the mortgages refinance them, so investors get their money back just when there seem to be no good fixed-income investments available.

Bonds may also be "called"—paid off early. This usually happens when interest rates have fallen and you're enjoying a high return on your old bond. Treasuries are rarely called; municipals, typically only after ten years.

But the chief risks with any kind of fixed-income investment are that interest rates may climb and that a company may have trouble paying its debt.

Fixed-income investments do best in times of economic hardship, when interest rates retreat, making existing bonds more valuable (because they are paying old, relatively high rates). During inflationary times, of course, existing bonds do poorly. In 1971–1981, when the consumer price index (a measure of inflation) rose 8.3 percent a year, bonds returned only 3.8 percent a year.

The best advice with regard to fixed-income investments inside a 401(k) plan is: if your nest egg is on the small side, play it safe. Stick to high quality and short terms. As you become wealthier, diversify. Buy a variety of different kinds of bonds with different maturities and different credit ratings. And as you approach retirement, move more out of stocks and into fixed-income investments.

25

MUTUAL FUNDS

Although people are deluging mutual funds with money, there's a lot of ignorance out there. One man has been heard to say, "I don't invest in stocks. Stocks are too risky. I invest in mutual funds."

Mutual funds are a way you can invest in securities—stocks or bonds, convertible stocks or convertible bonds, preferred stocks, whatever. They are like an IRA. They are the shopping cart; you decide what to put into them.

When you buy shares of a mutual fund, you pool your money with other investors, and together you hire an investment company (the mutual fund) to handle your money.

Typically funds offer these advantages:

- a diversified portfolio of stocks or bonds or whatever;
- a manager who decides what and when to buy and what and when to sell—and how much;
- analysts who do research and give advice to the manager.

The funds you can invest in via a 401(k) plan are "open-end" funds, where you buy and sell shares through the fund. You don't have to worry about the more complicated closed-end funds, which are really stocks that trade on stock exchanges. Their price per share, oddly enough, can be different from the actual value of the funds' holdings.

Broadly, mutual funds buy three different types of securities: stocks, bonds, and short-term debt. Stock funds may also be called equity funds. Bond funds may be called fixed-income funds (because "bonds" is a loose term, and because fixed-income funds may buy mort-gages—which aren't bonds). Funds that buy very short-term debt are called money market funds.

There are a variety of money market funds (Key 26), stock funds (Key 28), and fixed-income funds (Key 32).

You can make money from mutual funds mainly in two ways: from capital appreciation (the prices of the securities go up) and from interest (from bonds) or dividends (from stocks).

When funds sell stocks or bonds, they offer to send you the profits. Those gains, plus the dividends or interest, are called distributions. In a 401(k) plan, you would have those distributions reinvested in more shares. The combination of capital appreciation/depreciation plus distributions is called the "total return."

To evaluate the performance of a mutual fund, experts suggest, concentrate on its three-year and five-year total returns, then its one-year and ten-year total returns. One year may be too short a time to judge a fund; the manager may just have been lucky. Ten years may be too long; the manager may have lost his touch recently—or the manager who did so well years ago may even have left the firm.

Whatever the period of time, there are two main methods of judging a fund's performance. First, compare its total return over the years with the total returns of similar funds. You weigh the total return of a balanced fund (stocks and bonds) with the total returns of other balanced funds; you weigh a junk bond fund's total return with other junk-bond funds' total returns. This is how Lipper Analytical Services, a company that tracks mutual funds, evaluates funds. *The Wall Street Journal* uses Lipper rankings.

Another way to evaluate a fund's performance is to penalize a fund that has taken unusual risks to achieve a high total return—and to reward a fund that has avoided such risks and achieved a more modest total return. Risk is measured by volatility—by how much the fund's price per share (net asset value) has bobbed up and down. This is known as the risk-adjusted method, and it is used by *Morningstar* and *Value Line*, two other fund-reporting services. *The New York Times* uses the *Morningstar* rating system.

There is about a 60 percent congruence between the two types of rating systems.

Sophisticated, aggressive investors might pay more attention to the total-return method, conservative investors might pay more attention to the risk-adjusted method.

To check the records of the mutual funds offered in your 401(k) plan, you might visit a library to inspect *Morningstar* or *Value Line*'s ratings, or check *The Wall Street Journal*'s rankings. A fund in a 401(k) plan may not have the same name as a fund offered to the general public, but you should be able to find a similar fund from the same family, and check that fund's rating.

If a fund in a 401(k) plan is not evaluated anywhere, check its performance against an index of similar funds—a balanced fund against an index of balanced funds, for example. Again, you can find the performances of indexes in copies of *Morningstar Mutual Funds* in libraries.

Here are some sources of information about mutual funds:

- *Keys to Investing in Mutual Funds, Second Edition* (Barron's Business Keys, 1992), by Warren Boroson.
- *Morningstar Mutual Funds*, 225 West Wacker Drive, Chicago, IL 60606; 800-876-5505. Ask to see a free issue.
- *The No-Load Fund Investor*, P.O. Box 283, Hastings-on-Hudson, NY 10706. Publishes a monthly newsletter as well as a yearly book, *The Handbook for No-Load Fund Investors*.
- Mutual fund organizations distribute free or inexpensive literature. Write for the *Guide to Mutual Funds* from the Investment Company Institute,

1600 M Street, NW, Washington, D.C. 20036; (202-293-7700); *Investor's Directory*, Mutual Fund Educational Alliance, 1900 Erie Street, Suite 120, Kansas City, MO 64116; and *Directory*, 100% No-Load Council, 6625 Greene Street, Woodridge, IL 60517 (630-305-4600).

- Mutual funds also distribute free, informative materials. Here are the phone numbers of some large families: Fidelity: 800-544-8888; Vanguard: 800-662-7447; T. Rowe Price: 800-638-5660; American Century: 800-345-2021; Neuberger & Berman: 800-877-9700.

- If you have access to the Internet, you can check the Web sites of *Morningstar, Value Line,* and *The Wall Street Journal*.

26

CASH AND CASH EQUIVALENTS

The conventional wisdom is that everyone should have 10 percent of his or her portfolio in cash or cash equivalents, for these reasons:

- for rainy-day money. If the IRS decides that you owe back taxes and penalties, you are going to need money pretty quickly.
- for imminent major purchases—a down payment on a house, college tuition, a vacation.
- for opportunity money. If the stock market sinks, you may want to have cash to buy in; if interest rates start rising, you may want to have cash available to buy higher-paying debt.
- for stability.

In a retirement account like a 401(k) plan, the first two reasons don't apply. You should have cash or cash equivalents available in your personal portfolio, where it will be easy to reach—not in your retirement plan.

But the other reasons still are valid. If the stock market sinks or if interest rates start rising quickly, you may want to tilt toward having less money in stocks or bonds. A money market fund would be appropriate. Cash equivalents can also temper an otherwise aggressive portfolio.

Guaranteed investment contracts that mature in a year or less are cash equivalents. (See Key 33.) So are money market funds or money market deposit accounts (the latter are offered by banks).

The big advantage of money market instruments is that they won't lose any of your money—even if the stock market plunges or if interest rates climb. (Rising interest rates lower the value of most existing bonds.)

Besides, if interest rates should rise suddenly, money market instruments would catch up pretty quickly.

Money market instruments try to keep their shares worth exactly $1 at all times. They do this by investing in short-term debt, debt that comes due in, at most, an average of ninety days.

If interest rates suddenly bob up, a money market fund or account would lower the interest rate it pays in order to keep its price per share unchanged at $1. Then, as its existing debt instruments come due, the fund or account would buy newer, higher-paying debt and begin raising its interest rate.

The short-term debt that money market funds and accounts buy include bank certificates of deposit, Treasury securities, and commercial paper (the short-term IOUs of big corporations).

One money market fund actually lost its clients money. In 1978, a small fund, First Multifund for Income, extended its average maturity to over 600 days, then had to sell its securities at a 6 percent loss when interest rates leaped up. (Today, as mentioned, a money fund cannot have an average maturity over ninety days.) Other funds have come close to losing money. *Value Line Inc.* and T. Rowe Price Associates owned commercial paper issued by a company that defaulted, Integrated Resources. Both fund families voluntarily made up the losses, so shareholders were not hurt.

The shorter the average maturities in a fund or account, the more quickly it can respond if interest rates rise.

Anyone concerned about credit quality might prefer shares of a money market deposit account, which is what banks offer. These accounts are insured up to $100,000 per account by the Federal Deposit Insurance Corporation. But the banks' version of money market mutual funds has paid significantly less over the years—about 1 percentage point less.

Another way of raising the safety level of your money market instruments is to buy shares of a fund that concentrates on Treasuries, obligations of the U.S. government that mature in fewer than an average of ninety days. These securities are backed by the U.S. government. Money funds may also invest in federal agency notes, which pay somewhat more than Treasuries.

Despite the myth, some money market funds and accounts regularly offer significantly higher yields than others—chiefly because they keep their expenses low. The expense ratios of money market funds range from about 0.30 percent a year to 2.0 percent. (The expense ratio takes into consideration a fund's size: the larger a fund, usually the more efficient it is.)

To compare your money fund's return against the competition, check the newspaper listings. Large papers run a list of money funds and their seven-day yields, plus their average maturity, once a week, typically on Thursdays or Sundays.

Other types of money market funds include those that concentrate on Treasury securities, which are supersafe, and those that concentrate on tax-free municipal bonds, either across the country or just in one state.

27

FUND FAMILIES

A mutual fund family has been described as an investment company that runs at least one stock fund, one fixed-income fund, and one money market fund. In other words, it's a company that offers a variety of funds.

Your company's 401(k) plan may well be managed by a mutual fund family, like Fidelity or Vanguard or T. Rowe Price. Of course, many excellent money managers don't handle mutual funds for the general public.

If one or more mutual fund families are managing your 401(k) money, make sure that the family's individual funds have good records—and that any particular fund you are offered also has a good record.

You might visit a library and tabulate the average rating that *Morningstar Mutual Funds* gives the individual members of the family. You should also learn something about a family—its investment style, its strengths and weaknesses. Fidelity, for example, is justly known for its top-performing stock funds; Vanguard, for its low expenses.

Here are some of the best-known, most reputable mutual fund families:

- Fidelity Investments, Boston, MA
- Vanguard, Valley Forge, PA
- T. Rowe Price, Baltimore, MD
- Neuberger & Berman, New York, NY
- American, Los Angeles, CA
- Scudder/AARP, Boston, MA
- Strong, Milwaukee, WI
- Janus, Denver, CO
- Federated, Pittsburgh, PA
- Nicholas, Milwaukee, WI
- Franklin, San Mateo, CA

28

STOCK FUNDS

Stock mutual funds encompass what may seem like a bewildering variety of types, from funds that invest only in utilities to those that bet on the stock market's going down to those that invest only in indexes, like the Dow Jones Industrial Average or Standard & Poor's 500.

Unfortunately, the labels given to different types of mutual funds can be confusing.

The old-fashioned labels include names like "aggressive growth," "capital appreciation," "total return," "growth," "growth-income," "income," "equity-income," "special situations," and so forth. These weren't especially helpful: a "growth" fund might follow the "value" strategy, buying seemingly cheap stocks.

Also, how did a "small capitalization" fund differ from an "aggressive growth" fund? In short, the borders were fuzzy and so was what was inside the borders.

Then there are "global" funds, which invest in U.S. and foreign stocks—as opposed to "international" funds that invest just in foreign stocks. Puzzling.

Morningstar changed things a few years ago, classifying funds by what they actually invest in—large-cap value stocks, for example, or small-cap growth stocks. This was a big improvement. Instead of using the term "balanced" fund (stocks and bonds), it substituted the term "hybrid."

Here are the Morningstar classifications for U.S. stocks and their 10-year total returns:

Category	Annualized Returns
Large value	13.89%
Large blend	15.11
Large growth	17.44
Mid-cap value	12.01
Mid-cap blend	13.09
Mid-cap growth	15.91
Small value	10.63
Small blend	11.48
Small growth	16.50

Foreign stock funds are separated into: Europe, Latin America, Diversified Emerging Markets, Pacific, Pacific without Japan, Japan, Foreign, and World.

Specialty or sector funds are separated into: communications, financial, health, natural resources, precious metals, real estate, technology, and utilities.

Hybrid funds are separated into: domestic hybrid, convertible (bonds), and international hybrid.

Morningstar provides a style box (see Key 38) to indicate how a fund has been investing lately and uses letters to indicate how a fund invested in the past. Sometimes there's a conflict. In 1999, Fidelity Asset Manager: Growth was investing in "large blend" stocks according to Morningstar's style box. But the letters next to the name in *Morningstar Mutual Funds* were *LV*, for "large, value."

Still, while funds sometimes change their investment strategies, classifying them by how they have been investing recently seems the wisest course.

29

BALANCED FUNDS

If you have a limited amount of choices in your 401(k) plan and you want some exposure to stocks, consider a balanced fund. Such a fund is one of the best kinds of funds to own in a 401(k) plan, especially for fairly unsophisticated investors.

A balanced fund is typically 60 percent invested in stocks and 40 percent in bonds. (Morningstar calls them "hybrid" funds.) Actually, those percentages are rough, most balanced funds keeping some money in cash and varying the percentages between stocks and bonds. Many balanced funds have 50 percent in stocks and 50 percent in bonds. But a fund that has more bonds than stocks becomes an "income" fund. And a fund that has more than 60 percent in stocks is on its way to becoming an "equity-income" fund.

Here are some of the benefits of a balanced fund:

- You have a healthy exposure to the stock market, typically in conservative stocks.
- Your fund won't be as volatile as the stock market—in part because of your hefty dose of bonds and in part because of the conservatism of the stock-market component.
- You are less likely to lose money in a balanced fund than you are in the stock market. One reason is that stocks and bonds go in different directions about half of the time. And if the stock market goes sideways, you should have some income from the bonds you own (along with the stock dividends).
- A balanced fund will probably practice a passive

form of market-timing. If the stock market goes up and now constitutes more than 60 percent of the holdings, stocks will be sold and more money shifted into bonds. If bonds have soared and stocks have languished or fallen, the bond holdings will be cut back, and more money put into stocks. If both bonds and stocks have fallen or climbed in equal measure, the manager may stand still.

- The fund's managers may have the option to practice a slightly more aggressive form of market-timing, moving from 60 percent in stocks, say, to 50 percent. But this is fairly modest—and modest forms of market-timing are typically the most successful.

In the long run, you would surely make more money in an all-stock fund. But in the long run, you may have been so terrified by a sudden decline in the stock market that you moved into money market funds or guaranteed investment contracts. A balanced fund may not do as well as a stock fund, but it won't be as volatile, either.

30

FOREIGN STOCK FUNDS

Foreign holdings can diversify a portfolio, reducing its volatility; they can even zip up a portfolio's performance, because every year usually some foreign markets outperform the U.S. market.

Foreign stocks don't march in step with U.S. stocks, which is why your owning both can help stabilize a portfolio.

Here is how foreign stock funds have performed in recent years vis-a-vis an index of the U.S. stock market:

	Foreign Stock Funds	Plus/Minus S&P 500
1993	36.62%	26.57
1994	–0.61	–1.92
1995	9.65	–27.88
1996	12.06	–10.88
1997	5.34	–9.80
1998	12.68	–3.31
1999	50.93	29.89

In 1999, foreign funds finally reversed course and did better than the S&P 500.

Alas, most investors don't have anywhere near the 10–30 percent of their portfolios that conventional wisdom suggests that they have invested abroad. And maybe this is a good time to beef up their foreign exposure.

Right now, foreign stocks seem cheap compared with U.S. stocks, which have soared to the heavens recently and, like Icarus, may be getting too near the sun.

That's why the time may be ripe to make sure that your foreign investments make up a big enough chunk of your portfolio—that you have enough invested in international funds (which buy mainly foreign stocks) or global funds (which buy both foreign and U.S. stocks).

As William Holzer of Scudder Global points out, every seven or eight years the prices of foreign stocks vis-a-vis U.S. stocks fall to their lowest point. (Though he also points out that this could mean only that, from now on, U.S. stocks will simply decline faster than foreign stocks will.)

Are You Aboard Already? What about the argument that, if you own Coca-Cola, McDonald's, Gillette, and other multinationals, you're really already invested enough abroad?

Not true, argues John Bajkowski, senior financial analyst with the American Association of Individual Investors. "The riskiness of multinational firms is almost the same as that of purely domestic firms," he reports, "and their stock prices are tied strongly to the U.S. market." These firms, he concludes, "do not provide the benefits of international diversification."

Currency Problems. What about fluctuations in the value of currency? Jean-Marie Eveillard, who runs the SoGen funds, points out that if country A's currency loses value vis-a-vis country B's currency, country A may sell more goods to country B, thanks to their lower prices. So companies in country A may prosper and their stock prices rise, and maybe things will even out. (Eveillard has taken to hedging some of his portfolios, but he still has doubts about hedging.)

Funds can protect themselves against currency changes. "Hedging" means protecting yourself in case a currency becomes weaker. One way of doing this involves derivatives. You bet that Country A's currency will lose value—by buying a futures contract. If the currency does weaken, your futures contract makes money for you—offsetting some or all of the losses that you may have on any of Country A's stocks that you own.

Some fine money managers hedge their bets; some fine managers don't. It's a difficult, complex subject.

In fact, Christopher Browne of Tweedy Browne told

a conference recently that "We're never able to get the currencies right. So we hedge." Another speaker at the same conference, John G. L. Wright of Babson-Stewart Ivory International, echoing Browne, confessed he cannot accurately predict the direction of interest rates: "That's why we never hedge."

International or Regional? The conventional wisdom is that investors with small portfolios should consider a broad international fund, while people with sizable portfolios should zero in on regional funds.

The usual regional groupings include: Latin America, the Pacific Rim (with Japan and without Japan), and Europe.

What about international funds versus global? With an international fund, you can easily figure out what your portfolio's exposure to foreign stocks is. With a global fund, you give your portfolio manager the option to invest in either foreign or domestic stocks, whichever seems more attractive. Probably the decision is best made on a fund-by-fund basis.

What about single-country funds, most of which are closed-ends (sold on stock exchanges)? "They're almost the same as investing in sector funds," says Eveillard. "You have an extremely narrow focus. A regional fund gives you less of an upside, but less of a downside, too."

In short, when you buy foreign funds, you must make a lot of tough decisions. Choosing to be in foreign funds in the first place is only the earliest and easiest.

31

INDEX FUNDS

To find out whether Americans like a new television show or a candidate for President, a pollster will ask 1,000 or more representative Americans from all over the country for their views.

To find out what the "stock market" did yesterday, or all year, or during the past sixty years, a market analyst may check out a list of just thirty enormous companies (the Dow Jones Industral Average)—although there are 12,000 stocks that the public can buy or sell.

An index is typically a mirror of an investment market. It's a sampling of the stocks in various markets in the United States, or in the Far East, or in Europe. Or it's a sampling of the bonds in various fixed-income markets.

There are also indexes of small-company stocks, of transportation stocks, of health-care stocks, of real estate investment trusts, of gold stocks . . . the list goes on and on.

Indexes can also mirror investment styles. There's an index of undervalued stocks, an index of growth stocks.

Indexes are used to take the pulse of a market, to check what it has done—without someone's having to check out every single component of the market.

But indexes have another use. If you buy all the stocks or bonds in the index (or a sampling), your portfolio should do as well as the index—and the market. And you can actually buy an index—through an index mutual fund that mirrors a particular kind of market.

Large-company index funds are especially suitable for

- conservative investors—such as those nearing retirement;
- beginning investors—because index funds are

easy to understand and relatively safe.

Index funds have clear advantages:

- They are inexpensive to run. You don't have to pay a portfolio manager a lot of money to decide which stocks or bonds to buy. You don't have to pay brokers high amounts of commissions to buy and sell securities. (Indexes don't change their securities very often simply because the components of the index remain there a long time.)
- They are well diversified. While many mutual funds own a variety of securities, they may not own as many securities in different industries as an index. Many portfolio managers, in order to outperform an index, will emphasize certain sectors of the economy—and thus at times may be underweighted in, say, utilities or health-care stocks or financials. But while portfolio managers may beat an index this way, chances are also good that they will have erred—and will underperform the index.
- They do rather well. Because of their economy and their wide diversification, they don't just do average. They do better than average. The oldest index fund open to the general public, dating back to 1974, is Vanguard Index 500 Series. *Morningstar* rates its record, taking into consideration its total return and its volatility, as four stars—"above average."

Stuart P. Kaye, a pension fund manager, has adduced other reasons why index funds tend to do well:

- Actively managed funds occasionally lose their portfolio managers, who retire, go elsewhere, or die. The new manager may not be as good, or may simply follow a different strategy, which requires an expensive change in the fund's holdings.
- The assets that the manager handles may climb—and managing a large fund is a rather different ani-

mal from handling a small or intermediate-sized fund.

- Investment styles—growth versus value—go in and out of fashion. This means that managers may do exceptionally well when their style is in favor, exceptionally poorly when their style is out of favor. An index fund is a blend of styles, holding as it does undervalued stocks as well as the stock of growing companies.

But index funds have disadvantages, too.

- It isn't clear that all index funds, like foreign index funds, do better than actively managed funds.
- They don't do spectacularly well. They are never among the very top performers in any year.
- They are relatively volatile. A mutual fund modeled after the S&P 500, for example, will bob up and down more than a fund that also owns bonds—a "balanced" fund. (See Key 29.)
- They tend to give short shrift to small-company stocks. Most index stock funds are modeled after the Standard & Poor's 500 Stock Index or the Dow Jones Industrial Average, two indexes that are sharply tilted toward big-company stocks. Few index funds emulate an index of small-company stocks, like the Russell 2000 or Wilshire 4500, or even better-diversified indexes, like the Value Line Composite or the Wilshire 5000. (The Wilshire 5000 is the Wilshire 4500 with the 500 stocks in the Standard & Poor's index.) And small-company stocks tend to do better than large-company stocks over long periods of time.

The S&P 500, by the way, is a better mirror of the stock market than the Dow because its stocks are "weighted" by their "capitalization"—the number of their shares outstanding times their prices. The Dow Jones Industrial Average really is an average, and it's dominated by stocks with high prices.

32

FIXED-INCOME FUNDS

Inside a retirement plan, one of your goals should be to have conservative fixed-income investments: those with short maturities and high credit ratings. Short or intermediate-term Treasuries would be ideal; after that, short or intermediate-term investment grade (high-rated) corporate bonds.

As you grow more prosperous and sophisticated, you should consider spreading out—into longer maturities, lower investments grades, and even into such exotic fare as convertible securities and foreign bonds. As you approach retirement, move back to shorter maturities and higher quality.

"Short term" generally means up to five years; intermediate means five to ten years; long term means over ten years. As mentioned, the further out you go into the future, the greater the interest rates you receive but also the greater the risk.

Make sure that you know what the credit rating is on the bonds inside any fixed-income funds that you buy. You may not want to be buying junk bonds instead of investment grade bonds.

Make sure you know the average maturity (or duration) of the bonds inside any fixed-income funds that you buy. Otherwise, you may own long-term bonds when your preference would have been for safer short-term bonds.

Often an investor cannot tell exactly what he or she is buying from the name of a fixed-income fund—what the average maturity of a bond fund is, or what the average credit rating is.

Sometimes you cannot even know what a fixed-income fund is buying. Some funds that call themselves "government" funds own a lot of mortgage-backed securities, and they are not quite the same as Treasuries.

Below is how Morningstar Inc. separates the various types of fixed-income funds you might find inside a pension plan, and their ten-year annualized total returns.

Clearly, the longer the maturity and the lower the credit rating, the higher the return over time.

Specialty Bond	Return
High-Yield Bonds	9.77%
Multisector	8.13
International	6.59
Short-Term Bond	6.48
Ultrashort	5.92

General Bond	
Long-Term	7.74
Intermediate	7.26
Short-Term	6.48
Ultrashort	5.92

Government Bond	
Long-Term	7.41
Intermediate	6.75
Short-Term	6.34

Municipal Bonds*	
National Long	6.34
National Intermediate	6.08
Single-State Long	6.33
Single-State Intermediate	6.04
Short Term	5.22

*Individual single-state categories have been omitted.
Source: *Morningstar*

33

GUARANTEED INVESTMENT CONTRACTS

Some investors tend to heap scorn on GICs. "They are often riddled with high fees, the fixed-rates aren't inflation-proof, and the government doesn't provide a security net," writes Lee Rosenberg, a Certified Financial Planner. As for the word "guaranteed," he notes: "A guarantee from some insurance companies and banks today may be one step above a handshake." (He has in mind, of course, the financial problems of two giant insurance companies, Mutual Benefit and Executive Life.)

Other critics contend that too many Americans put too much of their retirement money into their GICs, meanwhile avoiding the stock market, which is where the real profits lie.

But a case can be made for GICs:

- They pay adequately—usually more than money market funds and certificates of deposit, and closer to short-term bonds.
- Most insurance companies are on a firm footing.
- They're not so conservative as money-market funds.
- If someone is unsophisticated and might become anxious and worried because of (perhaps only temporary) losses in equity (stock) or balanced (stock and bond) funds, GICs are a good, safe way for that person to get started.
- GICs can help shield a portfolio against too much

volatility from the stock market, volatility that could panic an investor into foolishly selling into a down market. If your portfolio is 50 percent into equities and 50 percent into GICs, you probably won't experience wild swings in your assets.

Just how much you should invest in GICs depends on your age, your sophistication, your overall wealth, and so forth. (See Key 37.)

The worst accusation that can be made against GICs is that the word "guaranteed" in their names is misleading. They certainly are not backed by the full faith and credit of the U.S. government, the way a bank account is (up to $100,000). Typically GICs are "guaranteed" only by the insurance companies issuing them, and if an insurance company goes belly-up, your GIC may be carried off to sea, too. That's why you or your trustee should periodically check the financial soundness of the company issuing the GIC.

GICs are like bank certificates of deposit. They pay regular interest for one year to five years. When the term of the GIC ends, it can be renewed at going interest rates. Like CDs, the value of a GIC doesn't bob up and down, the way stock and bond prices fluctuate.

Unlike CDs, GICs are not federally insured by the Federal Deposit Insurance Corporation.

GICs may have other names—stable value fund, fixed-income fund, capital-preservation fund, guaranteed fund.

How safe are your employer's GICs? One way of telling is to check how many companies are issuing the GICs: four to six different insurers or banks are desirable, not just a few. Then check into the insurers' credit ratings. Look for those rated "AAA" or "AA" by Standard & Poor's, Moody's, or Duff & Phelps. Ask your plan sponsor to tell you the ratings of the insurance companies issuing your GICs.

While banks cannot issue GICs, they can and do issue BICs—bank investment contracts. Unlike GICs, these are insured by the Federal Government up to $100,000 per account.

In the future, GICs may become more sophisticated instruments, actively managed to reap higher rewards from a variety of fixed-income vehicles.

34

LIFE-CYCLE FUNDS

For many investors, a life-cycle fund is the answer to their prayers. It's a ready-to-wear suit; a furnished apartment; an all-in-one portfolio. In short, the ideal investment for people who believe that they have better things to do than to follow their stocks and bonds closely—or who are eager to invest their money but are somewhat fearful and uninformed.

Life-cycle funds were launched because mutual fund companies learned that most people own just one or two funds. And if someone is going to own just one fund, it shouldn't be a sector fund, a small-company growth fund, an emerging-markets fund, or a junk-bond fund. The one fund should be well diversified— not just with different kinds of stocks (large, small, U.S., foreign) but with bonds as well.

The mix in a suitable life-cycle fund depends upon your age and your risk tolerance. If you're young and daring, you should be more exposed to the stock market (assuming that you don't have a short-term goal, like buying a home next year). If you're older and conservative, and in need of regular income, you should be more exposed to bonds and cash-equivalents (providing that you need income, and you're not really investing for your children or grandchildren). Cash equivalents: short-term bonds, for instance.

A life-cycle fund can be the core holding of a young person—and of an older person, too.

Some life-cycle funds become more and more conservative as the years go by; with other funds, you're expected to switch funds as you grow older.

Of course, if a person of, say, 50 becomes very rich

by age 60, thanks to his investments, he may want to become more aggressive because of his newfound wealth—despite his increasing age.

Fidelity Freedom 2030 Fund is for people who are planning to retire around the year 2030. It's a very aggressive fund and recently was 84 percent in stocks and 16 percent in bonds.

This one fund gathers together a variety of other Fidelity funds—U.S. stocks, foreign stocks, and fixed-income funds. As the years roll by, Fidelity Freedom 2035 will change its asset allocation and become more conservative. There are other Fidelity Freedom funds with different target dates.

Fidelity also has a more conservative version of its various Freedom funds, one that invests only in index funds.

Another possibility is Vanguard LifeStrategy Growth, the most aggressive of Vanguard's four life-cycle funds. It's normally 65 percent to 90 percent in stocks, 10 percent to 35 percent in bonds, and up to 25 percent in cash equivalents.

One of the four funds in this life-cycle fund practices market-timing: Vanguard Asset Allocation. The other three are index funds: Vanguard Total Stock Market, Vanguard Total International Stock, and Vanguard Total Bond.

One objection to life-cycle funds is that if you need cash, you must sell shares of the entire fund, both stocks and bonds, not just either stocks or bonds, as you could if you had a stock fund and a bond fund. You can't make a choice, selling stocks when you think they should be sold, selling bonds when you think they should be sold.

On the other hand, maybe drastically changing the asset allocation you've chosen for yourself isn't a great idea.

35

WHICH FUNDS TO BUY

The mutual funds in your 401(k) portfolio should be varied. They should cover enough different kinds of markets and different kinds of strategies so that, even if one of them fails you shamefully, the others will help carry you along to victory.

A panel of distinguished mutual fund investment authorities was asked: How many funds should someone own? The consensus: five to eight. (*The Ultimate Mutual Fund Guide*, Probus Publishing, 1993, Boroson.)

What general types of funds should you avoid? The authorities' answer was sector or specialty funds— although some of the experts would make an exception for such broad sectors as technology funds, health-care funds, and real estate.

Here are the types of funds that these experts believe that investors should have in their portfolios:

- growth funds
- small capitalization funds
- growth and income funds
- international funds
- equity-income funds.
- fixed-income funds

The panelists were somewhat skeptical about balanced funds, aggressive growth funds, and global funds (U.S. and foreign stocks). They were even more dubious about flexible or "asset allocation funds."

The sentiment of some of the experts was that certain types of funds don't have clear-cut guidelines, "equity income" being an example. In other words, the name doesn't convey much about the fund.

As for growth and income funds and balanced funds, the thinking of some experts was that investors should concentrate on individual funds—growth funds, income funds, stock funds, fixed-income funds, and not mix the colors on their palette.

Beyond the types of funds, investors should also check into the funds' strategies. It would be ideal to own both value and growth stock funds, for instance; funds that invest in big-company stocks and small-company stocks; and a variety of fixed-income funds, including high-yield bonds and foreign bonds.

36

SETTING UP A PORTFOLIO

What your 401(k) portfolio looks like—how much you have in stocks, bonds, and cash—is your asset allocation. The decision about how to divide up your money is not to be taken lightly. (See Key 37.)

A famous study (by Brinson, Hood, and Beebower, 1986) checked the performance results from ninety-one large U.S. pension plans between 1974 and 1983. The investigators examined how three factors determined portfolio results:

- asset allocation;
- market-timing; and
- choosing stocks.

What they found was that the first factor—how much the pension was invested in stocks, bonds, or cash—was by far the most important. In fact, they found that 94 percent of the variations in the portfolios' results was due to the asset allocations.

There is no definitive asset allocation model. With 401(k) plans, some of which offer only a few alternatives, you may not even be able to follow many of the more sophisticated asset-allocation models, such as those that call for foreign investments or even for gold-mining stocks.

Besides, even asset allocation models change over time. Older models allocate a lot to cash (money market funds). Newer models have tilted toward foreign stock funds.

Later Keys will describe conservative models, aggressive models, simple models, and complex models. You should choose a model that fits your age, needs, and desires, and stick with it unless your circumstances change.

37

ASSET ALLOCATION

Your first big decision was whether to join your employer's 401(k) plan. Your next big decisions are: how much to contribute and where to invest your money.

The way you invest your money—whether in stocks, fixed-income investments (like GICs), or money-market funds—is known as "asset allocation."

A sort of generic asset-allocation model is: 10 percent in cash (money market funds), 60 percent in stocks, and 30 percent in fixed-income investments.

The cash is there (1) to reduce your portfolio's volatility, (2) to provide you with opportunity money (if stocks fall off the table, you want to have some cash to buy in), and (3) to let you take advantage of climbing short-term interest rates if inflation comes galumphing back. (See Key 26.)

Fixed-income investments also serve to reduce the volatility of your portfolio. They also give you a regular, predictable return on your money, a return that's typically better than money market funds and Treasury bills give you. Over the years, bonds have done a little better than the inflation rate.

Stocks are where the big money is, which is why the ordinary investor may want to have some retirement money there at all times.

The trouble with stocks—and with the stock market—is that they can be volatile. The market lost 48 percent of its value in 1973 and 1974; it wasn't until 1980 that an investor in 1972 would have recouped his money. If you needed cash during that period, you might have been forced to sell some of your stocks—at a loss.

That's one reason you should limit your exposure to

the stock market: you might need money, and the market may be underpriced just then. Another reason: if the market went down and remained down for a few years, more and more investors would become discouraged—and sell. That would drive down prices even more.

Third reason: you might not be able to wait out a decline in the stock market. You're retiring next year, at 65, say. The market suddenly goes into a nosedive—and remains depressed for seven years. Could you wait to get your money? Would you have the patience? The courage?

The percentage of your retirement money that should be in a well-diversified portfolio of stocks depends upon

1. your age (the younger you are, the more you might have in stocks—because, not needing the money, you can wait out declines);
2. your overall prosperity (you probably can wait out any decline before you need money to live on); and
3. your risk tolerance or investment sophistication (in other words, the less likely you are to panic and sell when the market retreats). (See Key 19.)

There is no single "right" asset allocation for everyone. You have a wide lattitude of models to choose from.

Here's a worksheet to figure out your current asset allocation:

Asset Allocation Worksheet

CASH
Savings accounts   _____
Money market funds   _____
Treasury bills   _____
Subtotal $ _____ (A)
Percent of total (A/D)   _____%

BONDS
Corporate High Quality   _____
Corporate High Yield   _____
Municipal   _____
Foreign   _____
Treasuries, Savings Bonds   _____
Other   _____
Subtotal $ _____ (B)
Percent of total (B/D)   _____%

STOCKS
U.S. Large Cap   _____
U.S. Mid Cap   _____
U.S. Small Cap   _____
Foreign   _____
Subtotal $ _____ (C)
Percent of total (C/D)   _____%
Total Savings and Investments $ _____ (D)

38

THE STYLE BOX

The main reason why you should have a diversified portfolio is so that your portfolio is likely to remain stable. Even if part of it goes down a lot, other parts should remain up.

If your U.S. stocks take a bad spill, for example, maybe your foreign stocks will do OK, or your bonds. In other words, you want good investments that aren't correlated with one another—investments that march to different drummers.

What's so good about stability? First, it's psychologically comforting. If the loss a person has in stocks is scary, perhaps the fact that the person's bonds are holding up will be reassuring—and keep that person from selling his losers.

Besides, with a stable portfolio, you will have some money available for the unexpected—a financial emergency, perhaps, or a financial opportunity. You may not be forced to sell any holdings of yours that are temporarily depressed while they're depressed. Some may have held up nicely.

A stock portfolio of stocks or stock mutual funds can be diversified into five basic categories:

1. large-company stocks.
2. small-company stocks. Over many years, small-company stocks have done better—but erratically and unpredictably. That's why most authorities suggest that investors limit their exposure to small-company stocks.
3. growth stocks. Growth stocks are those of companies in good health, making more and more money.

They tend to be expensive, with high price-earnings ratios and high price-to-book ratios (standard measures of a stock's expensiveness).
4. value stocks. Value stocks are relatively cheap, often because the companies behind them have gotten into trouble. If you check back many years, there's evidence that value stocks have done better than growth stocks—but not in recent years. Value stocks are considered more conservative.
5. foreign stocks.

These five different kinds of stocks tend to perform differently year after year. That's why owning all five may bless you with a well-diversified, stable portfolio.

Ideally, your U.S. investment portfolio will have both large-company stocks and small-company stocks, growth stocks and value stocks. Morningstar, the publishing house in Chicago, publishes a "style box" indicating whether a stock mutual fund invests in large-company or small-company stocks, value stocks or growth stocks. The style box also carries entries for "blend" funds (both growth and value, or in between) and for "mid-cap" funds (between large and small).

The style box looks like a big tic-tac-toe box.

Equity Style Box

Investment Style

Value	Blend	Growth
Large-cap Value	Large-cap Blend	Large-cap Growth
Mid-cap Value	Mid-cap Blend	Mid-cap Growth
Small-cap Value	Small-cap Blend	Small-cap Growth

You can check with the mutual fund, or with *Morningstar* or the *Value Line Investment Survey*, to find out how any fund has been investing. Some fund managers do change their styles, but it's getting less common.

Generally, the more conservative you are, the more your portfolio should tilt toward large-company stocks and toward value stocks. The more adventuresome, the more your portfolio should have in growth stocks and small-company stocks.

You need not own funds or stocks in all nine areas of the style box. If you have a good blend fund, like an index fund of the Standard & Poor's 500, you don't also need a growth and a value fund. And if you have a good mid-cap fund, you don't need a large-cap or small-cap fund in that category.

39

MORNINGSTAR'S OWN 401(K) PLAN

As one would expect, Morningstar, the financial publishing company in Chicago, offers a fairly well diversified selection of mutual funds in its own 401(k) plan.

Here, as of 1999, are the choices among U.S. stock funds:

Large value: Selected American
Mid-cap value: Oakmark Select
Small-cap value: Fidelity Low-Priced Stock
Large blend: Vanguard 500 Stock Index, Domini Equity
Mid-cap blend: Gabelli Asset
Small blend: T. Rowe Price Small Cap Stock
Large growth: Harbor Capital Appreciation
Mid-cap growth: Brandywine, MAS Mid-Cap Growth
Small-cap growth: none

Among foreign funds, the only choice was Templeton Developing Markets.

No small-cap growth funds were offered as this category has done poorly in recent years. But a contrarian investor might have chosen at least one such fund for that very reason.

Doubling up on large-cap blend funds is sensible, given that this category seems to be the generic, plain vanilla choice. But the two funds are similar, Domini Social Equity being an "ethical" fund similar to the S&P 500, but avoiding tobacco stocks and weapons makers.

Some surprising omissions by Morningstar are the entire Janus family, which has shot out all the lights with regard to growth stocks; the awesome Franklin Mutual Series funds; and Legg Mason Value Prime, a sensational fund whose portfolio manager, Bill Miller, was named Morningstar's manager of the year not long ago.

Morningstar has noted that its average employee is only 30 years old, which explains why so few fixed-income funds are offered. PIMCo High-Yield, a junk-bond fund, did make the cut, along with PIMCo Total Return. Vanguard LifeStrategy Growth does have some exposure to fixed-income investments.

In compiling this list of funds, Morningstar emphasized depth of management and experience more than it had in the past, in the hope that a change in manager, or rising assets, might not drag the fund to the cellar. *Morningstar* also sought funds with low expenses, available especially to large companies via "institutional" shares. (Institutions include large pension plans.)

What is disturbing about Morningstar's 401(k) fund choices is how frequently they were bounced in and out. In many cases, funds were booted out because they had lagged behind their peers in their particular category. So, even if a large-cap growth fund had performed nicely, if it trailed behind other large-cap growth funds, it was expelled.

T. Rowe Price New Era, a natural resources fund, was kicked out because inflation seems to be no threat now; Liberty-Newport Tiger, a Pacific-Asia (not Japan) fund, was released because (in part) of its high volatility.

The other criteria that Morningstar used in choosing funds: the length of their track record; the length of time the manager was on board; the consistency of the fund's good performance; the consistency of the fund's investment strategy (not growth one month, value the next); low expenses; and "risk-adjusted" performance ranking. Volatility was punished and stability rewarded.

One more reason why a fund was added was to diversify the fund choices. Harbor Capital Appreciation was included because there wasn't a large-cap growth fund, and the same was true of Oakmark Select for a mid-cap value fund.

All in all, Morningstar was offering sixteen funds, only two of them fixed-income funds and only one a foreign fund. Seven funds had been retained and seven dropped. Four large-cap funds were available and only two small-caps.

The lesson seems to be that enlightened trustees of a 401(k) plan should be willing, like Morningstar, to change horses every once in a while. And that even Morningstar can make mistakes, not just in choosing funds but in not offering a well-balanced selection:

Offering its young, sophisticated investors only one foreign fund is clearly a mistake.

40

CONSERVATIVE MODELS

Here's a quick and dirty rule: A conservative asset-allocation model is one that recommends that investors over 60 (or close to retirement) have less than 50 percent of their assets in the stock market.

This extremely conservative model comes from the American Association of Individual Investors in Chicago:

Risk Tolerance	Stocks	Bonds	Cash
Five years or more from retirement			
Conservative	40%	30%	30%
Aggressive	60%	30%	10%
Close to retirement			
Conservative	20%	50%	30%
Aggressive	40%	40%	20%
At retirement			
Conservative	0%	50%	50%
Aggressive	20%	50%	30%

This model is derived from history—how much you can lose in stocks or bonds in any year. Other models seem to ignore the 1929 Depression, their creators apparently feeling that such an economic catastrophe is unlikely to recur.

Now look at this model, also conservative, from the Capital Consulting Group in Livonia, Michigan:

For Conservative Investors

Age	Stocks	Bonds	Bills
20–30	60%	20%	20%
30–40	50	25	25
40–50	40	30	30
50–60	30	35	35
60–70	20	40	40
70+	10	45	45

For Moderate Investors

Age	Stocks	Bonds	Bills
20–30	70%	15%	15%
30–40	60	20	20
40–50	50	25	25
50–60	40	30	30
60–70	30	35	35
70+	20	40	40

For Aggressive Investors

Age	Stocks	Bonds	Bills
20–30	80%	10%	10%
30–40	70	15	15
40–50	60	20	20
50–60	50	25	25
60–70	40	30	30
70+	30	35	35

To compare the two models, let's assume, in the first, that "five or more years from retirement" means age 50 to 55; "close to retirement" means 55 to 60; and "at retirement" means 60 to 65.

So, according to the AAII, someone of 50 who is conservative might be 40 percent in stocks, 30 percent in bonds; someone of 50 who is aggressive might be 60 percent in stocks, 30 percent in bonds.

According to the Capital Consulting Group, a conservative person of 50 might be 30 percent in stocks, 35 percent in bonds; an aggressive 50-year-old might be 50 percent in stocks, 25 percent in bonds. Thus, Capital

Consulting's model is more conservative.

Someone aged 55 who is conservative, according to the AAII, might be 20 percent in stocks, 50 percent in bonds; someone aggressive might be 40 percent in stocks, 40 percent in bonds.

Capital Consulting Group suggests that a conservative 55-year-old be 30 percent in stocks, 35 percent in bonds. An aggressive investor might be 50 percent in stocks, 25 percent in bonds. Here, Capital Consulting's model is more aggressive.

Someone aged 60 or more, the AAII suggests, might have nothing in stocks if conservative, and 50 percent in bonds; if aggressive, 20 percent in stocks, 50 percent in bonds.

Capital Consulting Group recommends that a conservative 60-year-old be 30 percent in stocks, 35 percent in bonds. An aggressive investor might be 40 percent in stocks, 30 percent in bonds. Here, Capital Consulting is far more aggressive. But it's still conservative compared with other models described in later Keys.

41

AGGRESSIVE MODELS

A crude but aggressive asset-allocation guide is: take your age, subtract it from 100, and keep the resulting number (as a percentage) in stocks. If you're 30, you should be 70 percent in stocks; if you're 40, 60 percent; if 50, 50 percent; if 60, 40 percent.

This guide has the virtues of

- simplicity;
- reducing your exposure to the market as you grow older; and
- keeping you modestly in the market in your later years, as you should be.

Below is another very aggressive model, recommended by *Worth* magazine. Allocations don't change with an investor's age. Everyone, it seems, should be 75 percent in the stock market and have nothing whatsoever in GICs and cash equivalents:

Diversified stocks or mutual funds	50%
Growth stocks or mutual funds	25
Bonds/bond funds	25
GICs	0
Money market accounts	0

Value Line, the financial publishing house in New York City, has carefully devised three asset-allocation models—for conservative investors, for moderate investors, and for aggressive investors. The more conservative a portfolio, of course, the less there is in stocks and the more there is in bonds; the lower the expected return; and the lower the range of volatility (standard deviation).

Conservative

Cash	24.13%
U.S. Bonds	13.69
High-yield bonds	13.04
International bonds	11.49
Large U.S. stocks	14.69
Small U.S. stocks	3.19
Foreign stocks	12.27
Emerging market stocks	7.49

Breakdown: Stocks: 37.64%, bonds: 38.22%, cash: 24.13%
Expected return: 8.26% a year
Expected standard deviation: 6.8

Moderate

Cash	0.00%
U.S. Bonds	8.03
High-yield bonds	11.22
International bonds	10.76
Large U.S. stocks	25.38
Small U.S. stocks	9.14
Foreign stocks	23.02
Emerging markets	12.45

Breakdown: Stocks: 70%, bonds: 30%, cash: 0.00%
Expected return: 10.2% a year
Expected standard deviation: 10.99

Aggressive

Cash	0.00%
U.S. Bonds	0.00
High-yield bonds	0.00
Foreign bonds	0.00
Large U.S. stocks	29.87
Small U.S. stocks	19.51
Foreign stocks	34.19
Emerging markets	16.42

Breakdown: Stocks: 100%, bonds: 0.00%, cash: 0.00%
Expected return: 11.54%
Expected standard deviation: 14.35

Comments: these are unusually adventurous portfolios. For a "conservative" investor to be 37–38 percent in stocks is a surprise. And having an entire portfolio in stocks is extremely aggressive, not just aggressive.

The stocks, by the way, should have been divided into value and growth.

42

COMPARING TWO MODELS

Asset allocation guides weren't handed over to humankind on the summit of Mount Sinai. Even two models, published in the same magazine in the same year, contain key differences—even though both would be considered aggressive (people over age 50 are urged to have over 50 percent of their assets in the stock market).

Here is one asset allocation guide suggested by *Money* magazine:

Ages 20 to 35

Large-company stocks	25%
Small-company stocks	25%
International stocks	25%
High-yield bonds	15%
Convertible bonds	10%

Stocks: 75%
Bonds: 25%

Ages 35 to 45

Large-company stocks	20%
Small-company stocks	10%
International stocks	20%
High-dividend stocks	20%
Corporate bonds	20%
International bonds	10%

Stocks: 70%
Bonds: 30%

Ages 45 to 55

Large-company stocks..15% to 25%
International stocks ....15% to 20%
High-dividend stocks 30%
Government securities..25%
International bonds...5% to 10%

Stocks: 65%
Bonds: 35%

Age 55 and over

Large-company stocks..15%
International stocks 10%
High-dividend stocks 35%
International bond 10%
Treasury securities...30%

Stocks: 60%
Bonds: 40%

Below is another asset allocation guide that appeared in *Money* magazine in the same year, a guide prepared with the help of the San Francisco investment advisers Bingham Osborn & Scarborough.

Single woman, 25, with $10,000

- stocks: 75% (large company 30%, small company 25%, foreign stock funds 20%)
- bonds: 25%

Differences from first model: This is identical with the other *Money* model, except that the large-company stocks have shed 5%, foreign stock funds have gained 5%.

Married couple, mid-30s, $50,000

- stocks: 75% (30% large-company funds, 25% small-company funds, 20% foreign stock funds)
- domestic bond funds: 15%
- foreign bond funds: 5%
- money markets: 5%

Differences: The first model is only 70 percent in

stocks, 30 percent in domestic and foreign bonds, and no money markets. The types of stock funds also vary: the percentage in small-company stocks rose from 10 percent to 25 percent.

Married couple, early 50s, $250,000

- stocks: 60% (large company 25%, small company 20%, foreign stock funds 15%)
- domestic bonds: 30%
- foreign bonds: 5%
- money market: 5%

Differences: stocks lost 5 percent, small-company stocks went from nothing to 20 percent, money markets gained 5 percent.

Married couple, early 60s, $350,000

- stocks: 40% (22% large-company stock funds, 11% small-company stock funds, 7% foreign stock funds)
- domestic bonds: 44%
- foreign bonds: 8%
- money market: 8%

Differences: stocks have dropped from 60 percent to 40 percent; bonds have climbed from 40 percent to 52 percent.

The point of this comparison, of course, is simply to demonstrate that asset allocation models are constructed by artists as well as by scientists.

ASSET ALLOCATION WITH FUNDS

The asset allocation model below specifies choices of mutual funds, so it is especially suitable for people who invest in 401(k) plans.

The options themselves include foreign, domestic growth, domestic growth and income, balanced, and income funds—five types of stock funds.

Fund Group	Conservative	Moderate	Aggressive
If your age is in the . . .			
20s and 30s			
Global growth	10%	20%	30%
Growth	—	25	45
Growth and income	40	35	15
Balanced	20	—	—
Income	30	20	10
Maximum in stocks	62%	80%	90%
40s			
Global growth	10	20	30
Growth	—	—	30
Growth and income	30	25	20
Balanced	20	20	—
Income	40	35	20
Maximum in stocks	52%	57%	80%
50s			
Global growth	5	10	15
Growth	—	—	20
Growth and income	20	25	25
Balanced	15	15	—
Income	60	50	40
Maximum in stocks	28%	38%	60%

Global growth	5	10	15
Growth	—	—	15
Growth and income	10	20	20
Balanced	15	10	—
Income	70	60	50
Maximum in stocks	18%	36%	50%

Paul Merriman, a mutual fund manager in Seattle, considers this model too conservative, pointing out that "under this scheme if you consider yourself conservative you are not allowed to have any, not any, of your money invested for growth once you reach the age of 40. For what is probably the majority of most people's lives, they [would be] shut off from participating in the long-term growth of equities in this country."

On the other hand, the model may be too aggressive in one respect: Nothing is allotted to money market funds.

44

REBALANCING

Let's say that you decide—because of your age, your risk level, and your prosperity—that you want to be 50 percent in stocks, 40 percent in fixed-income investments, and 10 percent in cash equivalents. You dollar-cost average your way into such a portfolio: invest in it gradually, perhaps over a year or two or three.

After your portfolio is set up, a few months elapse. The stock market has risen and the bond market has dipped. You are now 55 percent in stocks, 35 percent in fixed-income investments, and 10 percent in cash.

Obviously, your asset allocation is now riskier than you had originally intended.

Should you ride your winners and stick with your current asset allocation? (This would be the "buy and hold forever" strategy.)

Should you retreat to the starting line—sell enough of your stocks so you're back to 50 percent, and add whatever you've sold to your fixed-income investments, bringing that percentage up to 40 percent?

Should you put more money on your winners—invest more into stocks, less into bonds? Isn't it true that "the trend is your friend"?

Or, instead of waiting for a significant imbalance in your portfolio, should you automatically rebalance at regular intervals—every three months, every six months, every year?

No one knows the right answers, but the most sensible thing to do seems to be to rebalance whenever your portfolio gets badly out of whack. That way, you lock in your gains by selling whatever has gone up dramatically . . . and you buy securities that seem cheap.

A study by Stine and Lewis of Stephen F. Austin University published in the April 1992 issue of the *Journal of Financial Planning* concluded that rebalancing when a portfolio is a good distance away from its original is best.

The researchers had studied how various kinds of rebalancing techniques fared over three years, five years, ten years, fifteen years, and twenty years. The most profitable, they found, was rebalancing when there was a 7.5 percent to 10 percent misalignment.

"The passive portfolio," they wrote, "must be rebalanced to maintain a level of risk exposure consistent with the investor's objectives. . . . In most cases, the investor would be advised to rebalance only when the portfolio reaches a predetermined level of risk exposure rather than to make the adjustments on a calendar basis. This has the advantage of producing a narrower range of possible stock weights and, in most cases, requires fewer rebalances. . . .

"A reasonable strategy is to rebalance whenever the stock weights vary 7.5 percent to 10 percent from their original position. Over all the investment horizons, this strategy does better than annual rebalancing. . . . However, if the portfolio manager elects to follow a calendar strategy, rebalancing quarterly or semiannually is too frequent and the annual rebalancing strategy appears to produce the best result."

The Capital Consulting Group recommends rebalancing a conservative portfolio every year; a moderate portfolio every six months; and an aggressive portfolio every three months. The thinking seems to be that aggressive portfolios get bent out of shape faster than conservative ones. While that is probably true, a case can be made that the more conservative you are, the more frequently you should rebalance—to keep your portfolio more stable.

You will also be changing your asset allocation model as you grow older. You'll need your money sooner; you cannot wait so long for markets to bounce back.

When should you switch to a more conservative portfolio? You could set target days: your sixtieth birthday, for instance. But making such drastic shifts in your asset-allocation model all at once seems hazardous.

It would probably be more sensible to change your asset allocation more gradually. On your fifty-fifth birthday, perhaps, or your sixtieth, you might begin moving more into bonds and cash equivalents, for instance. And you could take advantage of high stock markets to sell stocks, and high interest rates to buy bonds.

To rebalance your portfolio, you can change your entire allocation by increments of 25 percent. Some plans will enable you to proceed more slowly—by changing the allocation of only your new contributions.

A study of real-world rebalancing conducted by *Morningstar* arrived at some interesting, persuasive conclusions:

1. Make sure that your portfolio is diversified in the first place. Rebalancing won't do you any good if your portfolio needs a new engine, not just a tune-up.
2. Focus on the stock/bond split. Getting the growth/value funds back in line, or the large-cap/small-cap funds, doesn't make as much difference as keeping stocks and bonds in sync.
3. Rebalance by the numbers, not by the calendar. Readjust things when a fund takes up 25 percent more (or less) than its original position.
4. Pay attention to taxes.

Don't rebalance so often; selling winners can cost you. Use new money to restore balance; buy your laggards, don't sell your winners. Or have your funds' distributions go into a money-market account, and use that for rebalancing.

45

DOLLAR-COST AVERAGING

If you regularly salt away part of your salary into a 401(k) plan, you are in effect practicing dollar-cost averaging. This is the case whether you are paid weekly, biweekly, or monthly.

Dollar-cost averaging (DCA) means investing the same amount of money—regularly. (Examples: $100 every other week. $1,000 every three months.) DCA works best with the stock market, because stocks as a group tend to bob up and down but wind up higher in the long run.

One benefit of DCA is that you won't buy a lot of shares of a stock, or a group of stocks, just when prices are unusually high.

There's another benefit.

Let's say that a stock is $50 a share in January, $100 in March, $25 in May, $20 in July. You're encouraged in March, and buy $5,000 worth of shares. You wind up with fifty shares. (Commissions and other costs are being ignored.) In May, your shares are worth $1,250 and you are worried sick. But you clench your teeth and hang on. "I'm a long-term investor," you tell yourself. By July, with the price down to $20 a share and with your having lost 80 percent of your investment, you decide to cut bait—and sell just so as to keep a measly $1,000 of your money.

Question: What happened to the shares of that stock in September?

Answer: That's unpredictable. The price may have dropped some more—or gone up—or remained the same.

But let's say that you decided to buy $1,250 worth of shares every other month instead of springing for the whole $5,000 all at once. You buy 25 shares in January, 12.5 in March, 50 in May, and 62.5 in July. In July you would have wound up with 150 shares, worth $20 each. You still have a loss, but it's only $2,000, not $4,000. And when you decide to hold onto the stock, or sell, or buy more shares, you'll probably be in a more composed frame of mind.

There's a third benefit of DCA: Even if a stock or mutual fund falls, you may make money. Reason: when you practice DCA, you buy the most shares when the prices are low.

Let's say that you buy $200 worth of shares of a no-sales-charge mutual fund every month.

Price Per Share	Month	Shares
$10	February	20
$5	March	40
$4	April	50
$6	May	33.33
$7	June	28.57
$3	July	66.66
$9	August	22.22

At this point, you decide to sell. Will you have a large capital loss—or, thanks to dollar-cost averaging, a small loss?

You started buying at $10 and sold at $9. But you bought the most shares when prices were very low, and bought the fewest shares when prices were high.

You spent $1,400—$200 for seven months.

The final price per share was $9.

You own 260.78 shares. At $9 a share, they're worth $2,347.02.

You have a capital gain of about $947.

Dollar-cost averaging has drawbacks. If a stock or a fund goes up, you would have been better off plunking down your money all at once.

If a stock or fund goes down and stays down, you would have been better off not investing in the first place and not dollar-cost averaging afterwards.

But the worst flaw of DCA may be that it's hard to get people to practice it. In February (in the example above), when the price is high ($10), they invest all their money: $1,400. In July, when the price is very low, they despair and sell out. Instead of making $947, they lose $980.

Recently, various academic studies have indicated that, most of the time, you are better off investing a lump sum directly in the market instead of dollar-cost averaging.

The trouble with these studies is that (a) they didn't consider the degree of loss you may have suffered when you invested at a bad time, and how long it would have taken your investment to heal, and (b) they didn't consider the danger that you might panic and sell after sustaining a major loss.

Let's say that you have all of your 401(k) money in guaranteed investment contracts. But you have now decided to move into the stock market. How long should it take you to dollar-cost average a large sum of cash or fixed-income investments into stocks?

John Markese of the American Association of Individual Investors in Chicago has said two or three years.

But if you are investing in a market-timing fund, like Fidelity Asset Manager or Vanguard Asset Allocation, you can certainly move faster. If you invest in a balanced fund (which has stocks and bonds) or a fund that tries to buy undervalued stocks, you can probably also move a little faster. There's less danger.

If you are withdrawing money from a 401(k) plan and putting it into another retirement vehicle, you can maintain the same asset allocation with your new portfolio. If your 401(k) plan was 50 percent in stocks and 50 percent in bonds, you can immediately invest the same way with a rollover IRA. You might want to use the opportunity, though, to modify your asset allocation in line with your age.

137

46

MODEST
MARKET-TIMING

One of the worst mistakes that investors can make is trying to time the market—trying to avoid bear markets and enjoy bull markets.

Most investors should simply follow their asset-allocation models, come heck or high water. They should not make sudden, drastic changes in their portfolios—for example, selling their stocks when stocks nosedive, moving into stocks as stocks begin to climb. There is even a term for what may happen to investors who desert one area that is doing poorly and flee to another—that suddenly begins performing just as poorly. Getting "whipsawed."

Investors should avoid aggressive, unrestrained market-timing.

But they might consider milk-and-water market-timing.

If you are convinced that the stock market is over-priced, or that the economy is going into a downturn, you need not bet the ranch. You can make small bets.

Let's say that the newspapers, magazines, or newsletters you rely on and people whose opinion you trust persuade you that the stock market is too high and you should take cover. Let's say that your portfolio is 60 percent in stocks, 10 percent in cash, and 30 percent in fixed-income investments. Here's what you can do:

- Diversify your stock investments more. For example, if you can invest in shares of a foreign stock fund but you own litle or none, move a percentage of your U.S. stock fund into the foreign stock fund.
- Move your stock investments to more conservative

stocks. Go from a growth fund to a growth-and-income fund or to an equity-income fund. You could move modestly: increasing your equity-income fund by 10 percent, shrinking your growth fund by 10 percent.

- Move more into cash. Shift your asset-allocation model from 60 percent in stocks and 10 percent in cash to 55 percent in stocks to 15 percent in cash.
- Move more into fixed-income investments. You could shift from a pure stock fund to a balanced fund, which has up to 40 percent in bonds.
- Practice passive market-timing. Just rebalance your portfolio whenever it's badly unbalanced (see Key 44) and invest regularly—so as to practice dollar-cost averaging (see Key 45).

If you practice these modest forms of market-timing, you may develop the courage you need to invest more aggressively in the stock market in general.

You might also consider such modest market-timing steps with regard to fixed-income investments if you think that interest rates are going up. You could invest more in foreign bonds, shorten your maturities, or put more into money-market funds.

47

WHEN TO SELL A FUND

Deciding to sell a disappointing fund is part art, part science.

Even sophisticated investors have sold poor-performing funds that quickly and energetically revived. Even sophisticated investors have held onto poor-performing funds that continued their wretched and miserable ways.

The fact is that it's difficult to distinguish between a fund that's suffering a few aches and pains and a fund that's headed for the morgue.

If a faltering fund happens to be in your 401(k) account, the decision to fish or cut bait might be more aggressive than if the fund is in your private account. With a 401(k) plan, selling the fund wouldn't subject you to capital gains, assuming that you have them. On the other hand, if you have losses, the fact that a fund is in your private account is an argument to sell it—a powerful argument.

A fund might have a good excuse: other, similar funds are also doing poorly. Maybe all foreign funds, or all small-cap funds, are in the same leaky boat.

Morningstar Mutual Funds provides a "category" rating of funds, indicating how well they have fared against their peers over the past three years. This might be more useful as a guide than the Morningstar official rating, which compares funds with only very broad categories.

Anyway, here are some reasons to sell:

- The star manager of the fund just left.
- The fund has changed. Perhaps it was once a small-cap fund; now that it's gotten successful, it must buy much larger stocks, or just many, many

more small-cap stocks. And maybe the manager isn't making the transition well. "With mutual funds," says Prof. Alfred J. Fredman, "success may contain the seeds of its own destruction."

- The fund is part of a family that has several other funds that are suffering—so this fund may not get the attention it deserves.
- The manager is new and his record is short.
- The fund has badly underperformed its peers—over the course of a year or more.

Here are some reasons to hold on:

- The fund has faltered before and bounced back.
- The fund family has a history of replacing poor performing managers—as Vanguard does.
- The fund family has a lot of gifted understudies waiting in the wings—as Fidelity does.
- A new manager has taken over.

Finally, keep in mind that you can hedge your bets. If you've begun to lose confidence in a fund, you can sell some of your shares—not all; or you can stop having more money invested into that fund.

48

CASHING IN YOUR 401(K)

Once you reach age 59½, you are entitled to withdraw the money in your 401(k) plan permanently, and without penalty.

If you are under 59½, you may be allowed to withdraw money from your 401(k) plan, and not pay it back, only for reasons of "hardship":

- to buy your first residence (not a summer home)
- to pay for college tuition
- to avoid eviction or mortgage foreclosure

You must prove that you have no other source of money. You must pay taxes on the money withdrawn, along with a 10 percent penalty. And some plans require that you not be able to make a new contribution for a year.

For more about hardship withdrawals, see Key 52. To borrow from your 401(k), see Key 51.

Someone can also permanently withdraw money for these reasons:

- death
- disability
- retirement
- termination of employment.

Avoiding the 20 Percent Trap. Let's say that you're retiring or leaving your employer, and getting a lump-sum distribution from your 401(k) plan. (A "lump-sum distribution" is just a big pile of your money.) And because you're under 59½, you would have to pay a 10 percent tax penalty on whatever you withdraw (along with current income taxes) if you don't roll over the money into an individual retirement account within 60 days.

So, not being immediately needful of cash, you roll over the money within those 60 days.

Unfortunately, that would be a mistake. Your employer would be obligated to keep 20 percent of your money—to give to the IRS.

You would get that 20 percent back later, when you proved that you did roll over the money. But in the meantime 20 percent of your lump-sum distribution wouldn't be earning a thing for you. It would be earning money for Uncle Sam.

There's something you can do: roll over another 20 percent of the distribution, using money out of your own pocket. In other words, you would receive a big sum of money—and have to roll over 120 percent of that.

Here's an example:

Let's say that on January 1 you have $100,000 in your 401(k), and you ask your employer for all the money. Your employer would withhold $20,000 and send you a check for $80,000. Now, to shelter your entire $100,000 payout, you would need an extra $20,000. If you don't happen to have $20,000 lying around, only $80,000 will be treated as a rollover, and the $20,000 remainder would be subject to taxes—and possibly to an early-withdrawal penalty if you don't kick in that extra $20,000.

If you do owe taxes on the distribution (because you didn't roll over all the money), Uncle Sam will use that 20 percent to pay the taxes you'll owe. You will also owe a 10 percent tax penalty for taking out the money before you reached 59½.

Fortunately, you can withdraw the money before you're 59½ without penalty and without your employer's withholding 20 percent if you're disabled—or if you withdraw the money not as a lump sum but in regular payments according to your estimated lifespan (in other words, as an annuity).

You can also avoid the 20 percent withholding altogether if you play your cards right.

You can arrange for a financial institution to handle

the rollover for you, via a "transfer," where the money is never actually in your hot little hands.

Ask a financial institution (like a mutual fund) to give you an IRA transfer form, fill it out, and obtain an account number—even though there's no money in your rollover IRA yet. Then present the form to your employer to transfer the distribution.

This option lets your retirement assets continue to grow tax-deferred. But don't mix up your distribution with an IRA you already have. Set up a new, "conduit" IRA. And don't ever add anything to this conduit IRA.

The National Center for Financial Education suggests that you have your distribution transferred into a government securities money market fund—the safest possible investment—while you ponder how to spread out the money into a well-diversified portfolio. You might have a good mutual fund company prepare the paperwork to accept your distribution into one of its government securities money market funds—although any mutual fund's money market fund or bank's money market deposit account would do almost as well.

Next, write a letter like this to your employer:

Rollover Letter to Your Employer...

Re: Lump-sum distribution from my retirement plan
                                         [*Date*]
Dear Sirs:
Please accept this letter as my specific instruction for you to provide the proper forms to me so that I may request a lump-sum distribution from my pension plan. I wish to direct my distribution funds into a rollover IRA account with [*fill in name of financial institution*] government securities money market fund [*or other money market fund or deposit account*].

Enclosed are the completed forms from the fund sponsors, so that they will be able to accept the check directly from you into a rollover IRA account.

The reason for this request is to keep you from having to send 20 percent of my distribution to the IRS, and so that 100 percent of my funds may be rolled over into the above-named account.

Please let me know if there is anything else you need to make this transaction occur smoothly. You can telephone me at [*fill in office number*] or at [*fill in home number*].

[*Employee signature*] _____
[*Address*]

[*Spouse signature*] _____
[*Address*]

Source: National Center for Financial Education, P.O. Box 34070, San Diego, CA 92163.

You have still other ways to deal with the possibility of your employer's sending the IRS 20 percent of your distribution:

- Reduce the withholding on your wages from the beginning of the year, while you are still working. That would partly offset the 20 percent withholding on your distribution.
- Reduce any estimated-tax payments you would normally make.
- Defer the distribution until the end of the tax year, and promptly file your tax return at the beginning of the next year. That way, you would get back your 20 percent as soon as possible.
- Leave your savings in your employer's plan. If your assets in the plan exceed $3,500, your former employer is required to let you keep the money there.
- Transfer your distribution into your new employer's plan. Some employers may insist on a one-year waiting period, in which case you might set up a conduit IRA (step 2).

49

WHAT TO DO IF YOU CHANGE JOBS

A study by Hewitt Associates, a management-consulting firm, has found that 57 percent of 401(k) plan participants choose to take cash payments when they change jobs—instead of rolling over the balance to IRAs or to their new employers' plans.

Yet surely the least desirable step to take with your 401(k) plan is to have your 401(k) money sent to you when you're changing jobs.

The drawbacks:

- Your employer must withhold 20 percent of your money for federal income taxes.
- If you are under 59½, you may be subject to a 10 percent early withdrawal penalty. You will also be subject to a penalty if you left the military service before age 55.
- If you are in a marginal tax bracket higher than 20 percent, you may have to pay extra federal income taxes on the money. If you're in the 28 percent bracket, for example, 8% more. If you're in the 39 percent bracket, 19 percent more. (Marginal tax bracket: the highest rate you pay.)

In sum, you could lose as much as 50 percent of your 401(k) distribution because of federal income taxes if you take the money out directly (20% plus 8% or even 19%, plus a penalty of 10%).

A better course is to keep your current plan with your old employer. Of course, you no longer will get any matching contributions. But you'll avoid current taxes and penalties. Other reasons to sit still: if the investment choices seem good, along with being well diversified. You may even be eligible for favorable tax treatment of the money: five-year averaging, where you can pretend you took the money out over five years.

But check whether you have easy access to your money. As a former employee, you may face certain restrictions.

Also preferable is moving your 401(k) plan to your new employer. One argument for this is that your money will be largely in one place. But you may have a waiting period before you can do this, and you may be forced to keep your money temporarily at your old employer, or in a rollover IRA. Again, compare your new employer's plan with your old employer's plan. Are there good, well-diversified choices?

One benefit of moving your 401(k) to a new employer is that you can discuss your investment choices with coworkers and benefit from employer-sponsored educational programs and materials.

A last possibility is moving your 401(k) plan to a rollover IRA available through banks, mutual fund companies, and brokerage firms. Again, you won't benefit from educational programs and materials distributed by your employer. But you will have a very wide choice of investments and a good deal of control over them.

Hewitt Associates gives these tips to 401(k) plan participants:

- Keep your money tax deferred. Even if it's a relatively small amount. A $5,000 balance would grow to more than $50,000 in thirty years at 8 percent. If you take that $5,000 as a cash payment, you may receive only $2,850 thanks to taxes. Assuming that you're in the 28 percent tax bracket, you add a 10 percent early withdrawal penalty and a possible 5 percent state tax.
- Remember: it's not just found money. It's not pennies from heaven. It's money to help you enjoy a comfortable retirement.
- Don't overlook the possible option of moving your distribution to your new employer.

50

WHAT TO DO WITH COMPANY STOCK

Sometimes it's better not to roll over your 401(k) investments into an IRA when you leave an employer—if your investments are in company stock. You may be better off keeping the company stock in your personal account, especially if the stock has gone up in price a lot.

True, you will have to pay taxes on the appreciation right now if you take the stock. Whereas rolling the stock over into an IRA would have postponed the tax bill.

But there's a quirk in the tax law.

When you receive your stock directly, you're allowed to pay taxes on your company stock at the (lower) value of the shares when you first got them—not on their (higher) current value. The appreciation will be taxed only when you finally sell your shares—and, of course, it will be taxed at a favorable capital-gains rate, probably 20 percent. Whereas, if you had put the stock into a rollover IRA and later withdrew it, you might be taxed at your top rate—up to 39.6 percent. This is a big difference, especially if a large amount of money is involved.

Some arguments for doing this:

The longer you hold your stock outside an IRA, the more that any rise in the stock's price will benefit from lower capital-gains rates. (Any assets withdrawn from an IRA, remember, are taxed as ordinary income.)

You can decide when to sell your stock. If it were inside an IRA, you would have to begin withdrawing your stock every year once you pass age 70½.

Keeping the stock outside an IRA means that your heirs will inherit the stock without owing taxes on any appreciation from the time you took the stock out of the 401(k) to the time of your demise. If the stock were in an IRA, it would be taxed at your heirs' highest tax rate.

Some arguments against:

If you're under 55 when you take the stock, you'll face a 10 percent penalty for taking the stock. If you plan to keep the money in a rollover IRA for a long time, maybe taking the stock isn't such a bright idea. The taxes you would pay immediately on the stock mean some of your money isn't being invested for a long time.

Keeping the stock outside the IRA means you'll have to pay taxes on the dividends every year. Inside the IRA, those taxes would have been deferred. (Any dividends, of course, may be small or nonexistent.)

Overall, *Kiplinger's Personal Finance Magazine* suggests that you keep the stock out of an IRA if you may need the money soon—to buy a business, say, or a summer home. Bypassing the rollover gets you the lower capital-gains rate.

If you won't need the money during your lifetime, taking this step can be a big favor to your beneficiaries.

Of course, you could compromise. You could withdraw all of your stock, roll over some of the shares to an IRA, and keep the rest in your personal account.

51

BORROWING FROM YOUR 401(K)

The cheapest place to get a loan is from generous relatives. The second cheapest is a loan that uses your home as collateral—assuming that you own a home. A good portion of the interest will be tax deductible (if you itemize). A third good source is your 401(k) plan, assuming that you really need the money.

Most 401(k)s let you borrow money, whereas most defined-benefit plans don't.

Perhaps 25 percent of all 401(k) participants borrow from their plans. That doesn't mean that you should—unless you know what you're doing, and you have a good reason.

The most common reasons people give for borrowing 401(k) money:

- to pay off other debts;
- to pay college tuition;
- for emergencies.

When you borrow from a 401(k) plan, you're really borrowing your own money. That's why you can get the money without a credit check and without red tape in general. And that's why the interest rate that you pay will be reasonable compared with general rates. (No, you cannot deduct the interest you pay.)

Payments will probably be deducted from your paycheck.

You cannot borrow all of your 401(k) money. You can borrow up to 50 percent of your balance that's "vested" (what you're entitled to if you leave your job). In any case, you cannot borrow more than $50,000.

The loans must be repaid within five years—unless you use the money to buy your main home. In that case, you can have from ten to thirty years to repay the loan, the time depending on the particular plan. By the way, while mortgage interest is usually tax-deductible, it's not if you borrow money to pay that interest.

Where does the interest go? To your own 401(k)—which means that you're breaking even (though your money isn't earning anything while it's out on loan). It's in effect a no-interest loan—not surprising, because you're both borrower and lender.

But you'll be losing the possible appreciation on the 401(k) money you withdraw. If the money had remained there, it might have made you a handsome amount of profit.

What if you take the money and use it as a down payment on a house? In that case, the appreciation you may have lost by taking out the money will be offset—in two ways. First, you will have less money to borrow for a mortgage (so you save paying interest on the money you didn't borrow). Also, with a larger down payment, you can perhaps knock down the interest rate on the entire mortgage.

So, is it a good idea to borrow from your 401(k) plan? It depends on how your 401(k) investments perform—and what you use the borrowed money for. If your 401(k) plan is all in low-paying money market funds, and you use the money to buy a car you need, for cash instead of borrowing the money, you may be ahead of the game.

But if the 401(k) money is in the stock market and you miss a swift, sharp rally, and you use the borrowed money to frolic off on a vacation, you will have in effect lost a bundle.

That's why, in general, it's best to borrow from the part of your 401(k) plan that's paying the least: a money market fund or a guaranteed investment contract.

What if you leave your job while you owe money on the loan? If you don't repay it within sixty days, it will be treated as a distribution. You'll probably have to pay income taxes on the money and—if you're under 59½ and not disabled—you'll also owe a 10 percent tax penalty for having taken an early distribution.

52

IN CASE OF HARDSHIP

A hardship distribution from a 401(k) plan can be made by someone with immediate and heavy financial needs. According to the rules, these needs must not be able to be met reasonably from other financial resources the person may have.

The plan must set up uniform and nondiscriminatory standards for hardship withdrawals. That is, the rules must apply to everyone—and not favor any one group, such as the wealthy.

The amount withdrawn cannot exceed the amount required to meet a person's immediate needs.

Some plans specify that only contributions that the employee has made can be withdrawn—not the earnings on those contributions, and no employer matching contributions can be withdrawn for reasons of hardship. Excess contributions—those that weren't tax deductible—also cannot be withdrawn for hardship reasons.

Even with a hardship withdrawal, if the person taking out the money is under 59½ there will be a 10 percent tax penalty. And the money withdrawn must be included as ordinary income on the person's a tax return.

A particular plan will describe what qualifies as a financial need. But the usual reasons are unreimbursed medical expenses, a down payment on a primary home, to prevent eviction or foreclosure, and for tuition for yourself or a dependent.

If you make a hardship withdrawl, you may not invest in your 401(k) plan for a year.

53

GETTING HELP

If you have questions about your 401(k) plan—the rules, how to invest, how to withdraw your money—the first place to go is to your employer's human resources or personnel department.

Your employer may give you literature to read. Or refer you to the investment adviser who manages the money, and agents for the adviser may answer your questions.

Other literature can also help. You might want to subscribe to various newsletters that report on mutual funds, or obtain the publications of mutual funds themselves, or of mutual fund organizations. (See Key 22.)

A good source of information is a web site, 401.kafe.com, where every week Ted Benna answers questions submitted by plan participants.

Ted Benna is the man who in 1980 noticed the provision in the 1978 tax law that led to the mushrooming of 401(k) retirement plans.

Among Benna's goals is to make 401(k) plans better—for example, by persuading employers to provide more options: "As plans mature and become larger," he says, "employers should probably be providing eight to twelve fund options, not three or four."

For tax advice, look for a certified public accountant, or at least an enrolled agent. A 401(k) plan may involve lots of money, and you may make costly errors unless you seek outside tax help.

For investment advice, consider a certified financial planner. Planners are usually better choices than accountants (unless the accountants have special training), stockbrokers, banking officials, and insurance agents.

For the names of CPAs who have financial-planning training, contact the American Institute of Certified Public Accountants, Personal Financial Planning Division, 1211 Avenue of the Americas, New York, NY 10036.

For Certified Financial Planners in general, write to the Institute of Certified Financial Planners, 3801 East Florida Avenue, Suite 708, Denver, CO 80210 (800-282-7526).

For fee-only planners, write to the National Association of Fee-Only Personal Financial Advisors, 1130 Lake Cook Road, Suite 105, Buffalo Grove, IL 60089 (800-366-2732).

Check whether the particular planner you are considering specializes in clients with money in retirement plans. Find out how long he or she has been in business (four years is a rough minimum). Interview a planner's references, a key question being: would you hire him or her again? Make sure that the planner's fee is reasonable. Be skeptical if the planner wants you to pay for continuing guidance.

In general, you shouldn't have to pay a lot of money for help in managing your retirement money. This book in itself should tell you virtually all you need to know.

54

ONLINE HELP

The Internet is a wonderful new way to obtain information, and investors in 401(k) plans are especially blessed.

Some 10 percent of all plans allow investors to go to the company's 401(k) Web site and check their holdings—at any time. They also allow investors to trade their holdings online. They may even provide advice to investors about their asset allocations—how much they might be in stocks and in bonds, and which particular stock and bond funds, depending upon their age, their risk tolerance, and their goals.

Alas, investors may be swamped with offers of help. One search has found 1,500 Web sites with retirement advice, along with calculators to enable the average person to figure out how much to save every year.

Two companies in particular, FinancialEngines and 401KForum, provide customized advice, in just a matter of minutes. They don't just give you cookie-cutter advice about how much you'll need to save. The fact is, saving for retirement is a very knotty problem. No one knows for sure, after all, how stocks and bonds will perform in the future. Both of these companies will give you probabilities, and they will even search through the funds offered in your employer's retirement plan to suggest what percentage of your assets you should invest in each.

FinancialEngines is available to anyone for $14.95 every three months. 401KForum is currently available only to employees of companies that have retained 401KForum.

FinancialEngines (financialengines.com), the brainchild of Nobel Prize-winner William F. Sharpe, examines a variety of possible scenarios. What if inflation comes galumphing back? What if stocks start providing only single-digit yearly returns? FinancialEngines considers such possibilities, then estimates how much an investor needs to save to reach his or her goals.

Whereas FinancialEngines provides customized allocations, 401KForum (401kforum.com) sifts through seventeen model asset allocations to find one suitable for investors.

When *Individual Investor* magazine had outside experts evaluate the advice given to one client by the two services, the verdict was: FinancialEngines was harder to use and gave more limited explanations of why it had chosen the funds it chose. But the experts decided both services were of great benefit.

Fidelity (PortfolioPlanner) and Vanguard (Navigator Plus) are offering similar services at their Web sites now, though both have drawbacks. Fidelity does not recommend specific funds, even specific Fidelity funds; and Vanguard will recommend only Vanguard funds.

55

THE HISTORY OF 401(K) PLANS

The first pensions for industrial companies began in Prussia in the 1860s, when workers started receiving benefits when they retired at 65. (Bismarck is supposed to have chosen that age.) The idea quickly spread to the United States.

In 1875, American Express Co.—not the financial services company of today but a freight service—became the first U.S. company to set up an employer-sponsored plan. Next was the Baltimore and Ohio Railroad, in 1880. Public utilities and banks soon followed suit.

Pensions became commonplace early in the twentieth century.

In 1926, the Revenue Act exempted from income taxes any employer contributions to pensions. In 1929, employer-sponsored pensions covered about 15 percent of private-sector workers.

With the Great Depression, many companies ended their pension contributions or scotched their plans altogether. Almost all union plans also terminated in the early 1930s. By 1938, there were only about 500 plans, which was 100 more than before the stock market crash of 1929.

In 1935, Congress passed the Social Security and Railroad Retirement Systems Act. By 1946, the number of pension plans had reached about 7,000, covering three million employees.

In 1962, Congress allowed the self-employed to set up tax-deferred retirement plans, called HR-10s or Keogh Plans.

In 1974, Congress passed the Employee Retirement Income Security Act (ERISA), which created individual retirement accounts along with the Pension Benefit Guaranty Corporation to insure the promised benefits of defined-benefit plans against the plans' being terminated.

In 1986, higher-income workers could no longer deduct contributions to IRAs.

The 401(k) plan was named after the section of the Internal Revenue Service code that authorized them, part of the Retirement Act of 1978. It was not until November 1981, though, that the IRS made it clear that employees could put pre-tax dollars of their own into the plans. In 1982, just 2 percent of the Fortune 100 companies offered 401(k) plans.

Effective on January 1, 1994, employers could obtain some protection against lawsuits from employees for 401(k) investments that performed poorly if they follow certain guidelines. To obtain this limited liability, an employer's 401(k) plan must

- offer at least three investment alternatives, not including the employer's stock in the employer's company, with different levels of risk and possible return. A guaranteed investment contract may or may not qualify as one of the three choices, depending on the circumstances.
- allow employees to make transfers between their choices at least once every four months.
- provide information regarding the objectives of each investment alternative, such as prospectuses and information about commissions.

QUESTIONS AND ANSWERS

Should everyone without exception invest in a 401(k) plan?

If your contributions are matched to any extent whatsoever, you should without question invest in your employer's plan. Otherwise, you are saying "No, thank you" to free money.

If your contributions are not matched by your employer, you might skip investing in a 401(k) plan if (a) you can defer a good deal of other income from taxation (via a Keogh plan, for instance, if you have self-employment income) and (b) if you are dubious of your company's plan because it doesn't offer enough choices or because your company's investment record is poor. (Even if the investment record is poor, though, you can always choose a conservative investment, like a money market fund or a guaranteed investment contract.)

If you feel that you can't spare any money at all, see if you can lower the tax withholdings from your salary check by increasing the number of exemptions you claim on Form W-4. After all, by contributing to a 401(k) plan, you will be lowering your tax liability.

What do you mean by "matching"?

Let's say that you earn $20,000 a year, and you want to contribute 10 percent of your salary to a 401(k) plan. That means $2,000 annually. Your employer might match up to 3 percent of your salary, dollar for dollar.

That means your employer would give you 3 percent of $20,000, or $600. So, if you contribute at least $600, or 3 percent of your salary, you will at least double your money.

What percentage should I contribute?

It depends on what you can afford, and what you want to save money for. If you're saving to start a business in a few years, or for a child's college education, or to buy a house, you probably shouldn't tic up much of your money in a retirement plan. While you can withdraw money from a plan in cases of hardship, you will have a 10 percent tax penalty to pay. Still, if you're saving for your retirement, be generous. People are usually urged to save 10 percent of their incomes. You might start with saving 5 percent, then bring up the percentage later on.

What's the most I can contribute?

Plans have their own maximums, but usually it's about 13 percent of your salary. In 2000, the highest amount of pre-tax money that you could put away was $10,500—not including your employer's contributions. Including those contributions, the maximum was the lesser of $30,000 or 25 percent of your salary.

What should I invest in?

If you don't know much about investing, start conservatively—with a money market fund or a guaranteed investment contract (GIC). A GIC is like a certificate of deposit offered by a bank, but it isn't insured by the federal government. In the meantime, read up about investments.

My 401(k) plan offers me a stock fund, a GIC, a balanced fund, and a money market fund. I can invest 25 percent of my regular contributions in each of them. What should I do? What's a balanced fund?

Decide what your asset allocation should be—how much you want in stocks, in bonds, and in cash or cash equivalents. The answer will depend upon your age (the younger you are, the more you can tilt toward stocks); your prosperity (the richer you are, the more risk you can take); your risk tolerance (which is roughly equal to your sophistication—how unlikely you are to panic and sell when the market goes into a swoon).

Let's say you're 30, you want to save for your retirement, and you've vowed not to sell in a panic is the stock market goes down and stays down. You might have 75 percent in stocks, 25 percent in fixed-income investments (like GICs).

A balanced fund is a good, solid choice for most investors. Typically it's 60 percent in stocks, 40 percent in bonds. So you enjoy a healthy exposure to the stock market, but have bonds for income and for stability.

What if I need the money after I've contributed it. Am I out of luck?

Most 401(k) plans let you withdraw money permanently, for hardship, or borrow money. Check your company's rules.

Could I lose money in a 401(k) plan? Could my employer keep my contributions?

Yes . . . and no. Certainly you can lose money. If you buy shares of a stock fund, and the stock market plunges, you will have a loss. If you buy shares of a bond fund and interest rates rise, you may also have a loss. On the other hand, you can't lose money in a money market fund and it's very unlikely you'll lose money in a GIC. But you won't make much money, either, in such conservative investments.

No, your employer cannot keep your contributions. It's your money, now and forever.

How can I tell if the company managing my money has done a good job?

Your employer should give you a report on the manager's track record—comparing the manager's performance with some index, like the Standard & Poor's 500 Stock Index. Another good way to evaluate a fund is to compare its performance with the performances of similar funds—a balanced fund against other balanced funds, for example.

If the manager also runs a similar public fund, you can check how the public fund has performed by examining issues of *Morningstar Mutual Funds* or *Value Line Mutual Fund Survey* in a library.

My 401(k) plan offers a foreign stock fund. How much should I invest in that fund?

First decide how much you want to have in the stock market. (The rule is that no one is brave enough to have over 80 percent in stocks.) Next, you might follow a rough rule: Don't have more than 30 percent of your stock portfolio in foreign stocks.

When should I change my allocations?

In general, don't try to time the market on your own. Even the most sophisticated investors sometimes get blown out of the water when they try.

Amateurs buy stocks after they have gone up for a while—and are overpriced. Amateurs sell stocks after they have gone down for a while—and are underpriced. Amateurs who determine to hang on through thick and thin are rapidly ascending to the level of sophisticated investors.

If you're determined to market-time, follow the advice in a reputable newsletter, like Standard & Poor's *The Outlook*: the front page of each issue suggests the percentages you might have in stocks, bonds, and cash.

Consider changing your allocation if it now differs

drastically from what you originally decided on. This "rebalancing" might take place whenever you are 10 percentage points away from your original allocation model. For example, if you set out to be 50 percent in stocks and 50 percent in guaranteed investment contracts, and you're now 70 percent in stocks, 30 percent in GICs, you might sell your stocks, investing the proceeds into GICs, until you're fifty-fifty again.

What if your financial situation changes—because you've inherited a lot of money, won the lottery, or landed a new job (and doubled your salary)? You can become a more aggressive investor.

As you grow older, become a more conservative investor. Gradually lower your exposure to stocks and beef up your exposure to fixed-income investments.

GLOSSARY

Aggressive growth fund   fund that seeks maximum capital gains. It usually remains fully invested in stocks at all times; it buys small, speculative companies and depressed stocks; and it may employ techniques like selling short and using leverage. Aggressive growth funds tend to be especially volatile.

All-weather fund   fund that does well in bull and bear markets.

Appreciation   growth in value of an asset.

Asset allocation fund   fund that either keeps a fixed percentage of its assets in various instruments—bonds, stocks, precious-metals stocks, real-estate stocks—or varies the percentages, depending on where the fund managers think the investment markets are heading. A true asset allocation fund has some investments in inflation-resistant hard assets (precious metals, real estate).

Balanced fund   fund that invests in both stocks and bonds—typically 60 percent in stocks, 40 percent in bonds.

Barbell   way of investing in fixed-income securities, so that short maturities are balanced by longer-term maturities.

Basic value investing   investment strategy that concentrates on buying seemingly undervalued stocks, based on their price-earnings ratios, price to book value, and other indicators.

Basis point   in bond yields, 0.01 percent. If a bond's yield goes from 10 percent to 11 percent, it has increased by 100 basis points.

Bear market   time when stocks (or other investments) keep sinking in value, despite occasional rallies, or when stocks remain at depressed levels.

Blue chip   stock of a large, prosperous, well-established company. The thirty stocks in the Dow Jones Industrial Average—including IBM, AT&T, ExxonMobil—are unquestionably blue chips.

Bond   debt instrument that pays a regular interest, whether or not the company issuing the bond is making money. Debt instruments are "senior" securities: their holders must be paid before a company pays owners of its stock.

Bond fund   fund that invests mainly in corporate, municipal, or U.S. Treasury securities. Such a fund emphasizes income rather than capital gains.

Bond rating   system of grading bonds on their ability to pay their obligations. Standard & Poor's ratings range from "AAA" (extremely unlikely to default) to "D" (in default). Moody's ratings are similar.

Bottom up method of investing in which the investor concentrates on buying attractive stocks, whatever the broad trends of the market or the economy. *See* **Top down**.

Broker/dealer firm, like Merrill Lynch, that buys and sells load mutual funds and other securities to the public.

Bull market time when stocks (or other securities) keep climbing in value, despite occasional stumbles. Sometimes the boundary between bull and bear markets isn't sharp.

Bullet way of investing in fixed-income securities in which the maturities are neither short term nor long term but intermediate term.

Buy and hold investment strategy that entails buying shares of stock or a mutual fund for the long term and selling them only in special circumstances, such as after a long-term loss. *See* **Market timing**.

Cash equivalents short-term obligations, like Treasury bills.

Certificates of deposit conservative debt instruments provided by a bank or savings and loan, with maturities varying from months to several years. Usually there are penalties if an investor cashes in a CD before maturity. With a floating rate CD, the interest rate changes in line with the prime rate, the rate for favored borrowers.

Common stock security representing ownership of a public corporation's assets.

Contribution money you put into a retirement plan.

Corporate bond fund fund that invests in corporate bonds, which may be high rated or low rated, and have short-term, medium-term, or long-term maturities.

Current yield dividends paid to investors, expressed as a percentage of the current price.

Defined benefit plan retirement plan in which an employer is responsible for investing employees' money. *See* **Defined contribution plan**.

Defined contribution plan retirement plan, like a 401(k), that allows employees to invest pre-tax money for their retirement. Their contributions are limited ("defined"). Employees manage their own investments. *See* **Defined benefit plan**.

Distributions payments that a mutual fund makes to its shareholders, from the sales of its securities, from interest, from dividends—or a return of the shareholder's original investment.

Diversification spreading investments over a variety of different securities, to reduce risk.

Dividends money (or stock) that a company pays the owners of its stock, usually four times a year.

Dollar-cost averaging investing the same amount of money at regular intervals, so that when securities are low-priced you buy more shares. A method of diversifying the prices at which you buy securities.

Dow Jones Industrial Average model for the stock market as a whole. It consists of thirty blue-chip stocks.

Equities stocks, real estate, other assets that an investor owns, as opposed to bonds, where an investor lends money.

Equity-income type of mutual fund that concentrates on high-paying common stocks.

Event risk the danger that a bond will lose value because of special situations, such as the issuer being subjected to a leveraged buyout and acquiring a great deal of new debt.

Fair-weather fund fund that excels in bull markets but gives a mediocre or poor performance in bear markets. *See* **Foul-weather fund**.

Family group of mutual funds under one umbrella, typically consisting of a stock fund, a bond fund, and a money market fund.

Fixed-income fund fund that invests mainly in bonds and preferred stock.

Flexible *See* **asset allocation**.

Formula investing investing according to mechanical techniques, such as dollar-cost averaging.

Foul-weather fund fund that excels in bear markets, one explanation being that the fund invests in securities that are already undervalued. *See* **Fair-weather fund**.

401(k) plan retirement plan set up by an employer that allows employees to set aside a certain percentage of their salaries, before taxes, for retirement. Often the employer matches the employees' contributions up to a point.

403(b) plan retirement plan for employees of public institutions, like schools.

General obligation bonds bonds that pay holders from their basic taxing authority—as opposed to revenue bonds.

Global fund one that invests in foreign as well as domestic stocks.

GNMA fund fund that invests in mortgage securities issued by the Government National Mortgage Association.

Government bond fund fund that invests mostly in Treasuries, but also possibly in government agency bonds and mortgage-backed securities.

Growth and income fund fund that invests in growth stocks as well as high-income, blue chip stocks.

Growth fund fund that invests in companies that seem to have bright futures in view of their growth rates.

Guaranteed investment contract investment, like a certificate of deposit, offered by an insurance company for 401(k) investors.

Hedge fund fund that not only invests in securities but may also sell short or write options, in order to protect itself from losses.

Income fund fund that stresses current income rather than growth of capital. Such funds may be invested in high-yielding stocks and in bonds, but mainly in bonds.

Index model of an investment market—stocks, bonds, utilities, health-care stocks, and so forth.

Index fund fund that attempts to emulate the performance of an index, like the Standard & Poor's 500 or the Shearson-Lehman Bond Index.

Individual retirement account (IRA) retirement plan that enables relatively low-income employees, or those with no pension coverage, to save up to $2,000 a year tax free.

Interest   regular payments from a borrower to a lender in return for the loan.

International fund   fund that invests in the securities of foreign corporations or governments.

Investment grade bonds   bonds rated "BBB," Standard & Poor's fourth-highest category, and above.

Investment objectives   goals of a mutual fund, such as long-term capital gains, with income secondary.

Junk bonds   bonds rated "BB" or below by Standard & Poor's. Such bonds are not so safe as investment grade bonds, but they pay higher interest. Also called "high yield bonds."

Ladder   arranging the maturities of one's fixed-income investments so they become due at different times—such as one year, two years, and three years.

Life-cycle fund   a fund that matches the investor with a portfolio suitable for his age, goals, or risk tolerance.

Liquidity   measure of how readily an asset can be sold for cash. If an asset can readily be sold, but at a loss, its liquidity is compromised. In this respect, a money market fund is far more liquid than a stock fund.

Market-timing   attempting to buy securities near the end of a bear market and to sell them near the end of a bull market—in other words, to buy low and sell high. *See* **Buy and hold**.

Maturity   when a loan—or a bond—is due to be paid off by the debtor or by the issuing company.

Money market fund   fund that invests in debt obligations with average maturities of no more than ninety days. To keep the principal unchanging, usually at $1 a share, the fund varies the yield. Banks' funds are called money market deposit accounts.

Mortgage-backed securities   shares of a pool of mortgages, issued by Fannie Mae (Federal National Mortgage Association), Freddie Mac (Federal Home Loan Mortgage Corporation), or Ginnie Mae (Government National Mortgage Association). Investors receive regular payments of principal and interest from the underlying mortgages.

Net asset value   price per share of a fund: the fund's net assets divided by the number of shares outstanding.

Net assets   value of a fund's holdings, minus debts, such as taxes owed.

No-load   fund that does not charge a front-end commission. A "pure" no-load also has no deferred sales charge, and typically no redemption fee and no 12b-1 fee.

Open-end investment company   fund that can continually issue more shares and thus add to its net assets. Such a fund also buys shares directly from its customers and sells shares directly to its customers. *See* **Closed-end investment company**.

Over-the-counter   market in which securities are bought and sold through dealers, not on the floor of an exchange. OTC stocks are typically those of smaller companies.

Performance how well a fund has fared over a certain period of time, usually measured by capital gains, dividends, and interest the fund has earned.

Portfolio various securities held by an individual or a fund.

Portfolio manager person or committee that makes buy-and-sell decisions for a fund.

Premium percentage by which a security's price exceeds its net asset value per share. A bond paying high interest may trade at a premium.

Price-earnings ratio price per share of a stock, divided by its last twelve months of earnings (or estimated earnings for the next year). The P/E ratio indicates a stock's popularity by reflecting how much investors are willing to pay for its earning power.

Prospectus official document describing a mutual fund. It must be furnished to investors.

Qualified retirement plan with contributions that are tax-deferred.

Rebalancing changing one's assets allocation back to the original model after it has deviated. If the model allocation was 50 percent stocks, 40 percent bonds, and 10 percent cash, the portfolio might be rebalanced if the percentages changed over time.

Redemption fee charge a fund may levy, especially if an investor sells shares purchased recently.

Revenue bonds bonds that pay their holders from money the issuer earns—as from a turnpike authority—rather than from taxes.

Risk either the volatility of an instrument, or the possibility that the investment will lose value.

Risk tolerance ability of a person to accept what may be temporary losses from an investment.

Sales charge commission an investor must pay to buy shares of certain load mutual funds or of a limited partnership.

Sector stocks in one industry.

Secular long-term.

Securities stocks, bonds, options, warrants, or other instruments that signify a corporation's obligations to an investor.

Securities and Exchange Commission (SEC) federal agency, created in 1934, that administers the securities laws.

Small-company fund fund of small-company stocks—the size usually being measured in terms of capitalization, which is stock price times shares outstanding.

Specialty fund that restricts its horizon to certain stocks: health care, regional banks, utilities, gold, and so forth.

Spread difference between the bid and the offer prices on a stock or bond.

Standard & Poor's 500 popular microcosm of the stock market, based on the prices of 500 widely held common stocks.

Standard deviation volatility of an investment, measured by comparing its average price with the degree of its ups and downs.

Stock *see* **Common stock.**

Time horizon   how long you can remain invested before you will need your principal. The longer your time horizon, the greater the chance that you will escape needing your money in a down market

Top down   method of investing in which the investor looks at general economic trends, then decides which industries and companies will benefit. *See* **Bottom up**.

Total return   profit or loss that a mutual fund has achieved over a period of time, including capital gains or losses, interest and dividends, and expenses. It is expressed as a percentage of the original value of the assets.

Treasury   debts of the U.S. government. The maturities of Treasury bills are up to one year, of notes, two to ten years, and of bonds, ten to thirty years.

Turnover ratio   trading activity of a mutual fund, calculated by dividing the lesser of purchases or sales for the fund's fiscal year by the monthly average of the portfolio's net assets. Excluded are securities that mature within a year. A turnover ratio of 100 percent is the equivalent of a complete portfolio turnover.

12b-1 fee   amount that a fund takes from its assets—and thus from its shareholders—to pay for distribution and marketing costs. Usually .25 percent to 1.25 percent of assets. Also called a hidden load.

Unit investment trust   fund that buys a portfolio of securities—usually bonds—and normally holds them until maturity.

Volatility   fluctuations in the price of a security or index of securities.

Will   legal document that provides for how your assets are transferred on your death.

Wilshire 5000   model of all stocks, including those on the New York Stock Exchange, the American Exchange, and over-the-counter. The Wilshire is one of the broadest indexes, and includes over 6,000 stocks.

Yield   regular income from a fund, expressed as a percentage of the fund's average net asset value, not including capital gains or losses.

Yield curve   graph comparing the interest rates of similar bonds according to their maturities. Usually long-term rates are higher than short-term rates. When short-term rates are higher, there is an "inverted" yield curve.

Yield to maturity   yield (as above) plus any certain gians or loss on the price of a bond from now until the time it comes due, expressed as a percentage of the bond's price.

Zero coupon bond   bond sold at a fraction of its face value. Its value gradually appreciates as its maturity approaches. No interest is paid to investors, but they must nonetheless pay taxes on the interest accruing annually (except for tax-exempt bonds). Earnings accumulate until maturity.

INDEX

BARRON'S BUSINESS KEYS Each "key" explains approximately 50 concepts and provides a glossary and index. Each book: Paperback, approx. 160 pp., 4³⁄₁₆" x 7", $4.95, $5.95, & $7.95 Can. $6.50, $7.95, $8.50, & $11.50.

Keys for Women Starting or Owning a Business (4609-9)
Keys to Avoiding Probate and Reducing Estate Taxes (4668-4)
Keys to Business and Personal Financial Statements (4622-6)
Keys to Buying Foreclosed and Bargain Homes, 2nd *(1294-5)
Keys to Buying a Franchise (4484-3)
Keys to Buying and Owning a Home, 3rd Edition *(1299-6)
Keys to Buying and Selling a Business (4430-4)
Keys to Conservative Investments, 2nd Edition (9006-3)
Keys to Improving Your Return on Investments (ROI) (4641-2)
Keys to Incorporating, 2nd Edition (9055-1)
Keys to Investing in Common Stocks, 3rd Edition *(1301-1)
Keys to Investing in Corporate Bonds (4386-3)
Keys to Investing in Government Securities, 2nd Edition (9150-7)
Keys to Investing in International Stocks (4759-1)
Keys to Investing in Municipal Bonds (9515-4)
Keys to Investing in Mutual Funds, 3rd Edition (9644-4)
Keys to Investing in Options and Futures, 3rd Edition *(1303-8)
Keys to Investing in Real Estate, 3rd Edition *(1295-3)
Keys to Investing in Your 401(K), 2nd Edition *(1298-8)
Keys to Managing Your Cash Flow (4755-9)
Keys to Mortgage Financing and Refinancing, 2nd Edition (1436-7)
Keys to Personal Financial Planning, 2nd Edition (1919-9)
Keys to Personal Insurance (4922-5)
Keys to Purchasing a Condo or a Co-op, 2nd Edition *(1305-4)
Keys to Reading an Annual Report, 2nd Edition (9240-6)
Keys to Retirement Planning, 2nd Edition (9013-6)
Keys to Risks and Rewards of Penny Stocks (4300-6)
Keys to Saving Money on Income Taxes, 2nd Edition (9012-8)
Keys to Starting a Small Business (4487-8)
Keys to Starting an Export Business (9600-2)
Keys to Surviving a Tax Audit (4513-0)
Keys to Understanding the Financial News, 3rd Edition *(1308-9)
Keys to Understanding Securities, 2nd Edition *(1309-7)

Available at bookstores, or by mail from Barron's. Enclose check or money order for full amount plus sales tax where applicable and 18% for postage & handling (minimum charge $5.95). Prices subject to change without notice. $= U.S. dollars • Can. $= Canadian dollars • Barron's ISBN Prefix 0-8120, *indicates 0-7641

Barron's Educational Series, Inc.
250 Wireless Boulevard • Hauppauge, NY 11788
In Canada: Georgetown Book Warehouse
34 Armstrong Avenue, Georgetown, Ont. L7G 4R9
www.barronseduc.com